KS2 GRAMMAR
PUNCTUATION & SPELLING
SATs SUCCESS
WORKBOOK

SHELLEY WELSH

Getting the most out of this book

Practise every topic with tons of questions

Get fully prepared with the SATs questions at the back

You'll find 'Top tips' along the way to help you do your best

Use the answers to see how well you're doing

Dear grown-ups,

This book is supposed to be an enjoyable learning experience - so help your child to see it that way! Do not let them plough through in one go - remember the 'little and often' rule. This way, your child will not see it as a chore and it will be more effective.

Use the Letts KS2 Success Grammar, Punctuation & Spelling Revision Guide (ISBN 9781844199259) alongside this workbook to help you prepare for the test.

Contents

Grammar Terms

Nouns 4
Verbs 6
Modal verbs 8
Adjectives 10
Conjunctions 12
Pronouns 14
Adverbs and adverbials 16
Prepositions 18
Determiners 20

Creating Sentences

Phrases and clauses 22
Relative clauses 24
Sentence types 26

Sentence Features

Subject–Verb agreement 28
Subject and object 30
Active and passive voice 32
Direct speech 34
Informal and formal speech 36

Punctuation

Capital letters and full stops 38

Question marks and exclamation marks 40

Commas 42

Inverted commas 44

Apostrophes 46

Punctuation to indicate parenthesis 48

Colons, semi-colons, dashes and bullet points 50

Hyphens and ellipses 52

Vocabulary and Spelling

Synonyms and antonyms 54

Prefixes 56

Suffixes 58

Tricky spellings 62

Tricky plurals 66

Homophones 68

SATs Practice Questions 70

Glossary 79

Answers 1–16
Set in a pull-out booklet in the centre of the book

Nouns

1 Underline the common **nouns** in these sentences.

a. We ate the pizza and drank our juice. **(1 mark)**

b. She swapped her book at the library. **(1 mark)**

c. He dropped lots of pencils on the floor. **(1 mark)**

d. The girls stopped talking and listened to their teacher. **(1 mark)**

e. Our school closed early because of the heavy snow. **(1 mark)**

f. Scarves, gloves and hats – all were packed for the trip. **(1 mark)**

Noun types

1 Explain why some of the words in this sentence start with a capital letter. **(1 mark)**

Last August, when Emilie went on holiday to Spain, she read *The Chronicles of Narnia.*

Last is the start of the sentence. August is a time. Emilie is a name. Spain is a place. The Chronicles of Narnia is a book title

2 Underline **all** the common and proper nouns in the following sentences.

a. The ducks wandered down the road and into the field. **(1 mark)**

b. Our team finished early on Wednesday because of the snow. **(1 mark)**

c. Phil showed great courage when faced with the tiger. **(1 mark)**

d. Prince William visited Wales at the beginning of July. **(1 mark)**

e. My football hit the top bar of the net. **(1 mark)**

f. We went in the sea, although the weather was grim and the waves rough. **(1 mark)**

Expanded noun phrases

1 Underline all the **expanded noun phrases** in the following sentences.

a. The <u>beautiful blue butterfly</u> landed on my bare shoulder. **(1 mark)**

b. We showed a lot of courage in spite of the <u>awful danger</u> we were in. **(1 mark)**

c. My old grandfather kept two herds of cows on his five-acre farm. **(1 mark)**

d. Our local primary school has a well-stocked library full of interesting books. **(1 mark)**

e. Sasha went to the beautiful islands of Guernsey and Jersey for his first-ever holiday. **(1 mark)**

f. After eating cheese and ham sandwiches, my little sister and I headed home. **(1 mark)**

2 Add suitable determiners and adjectives to these nouns to create expanded noun phrases.
An example has been done for you. **(5 marks)**

puppy	The mischievous little puppy.
countryside	....
determination	....
disgust	....
ocean	....
swarm	....

Remind your child that names of planets, mountains, rivers, countries, book titles, months of the year and days of the week are all proper nouns and therefore start with a capital letter.

Parent tip!

Total $\frac{}{24}$

Identifying verbs

❶ Underline the **verbs** in these sentences.
There may be more than one in each.

    a. The fire roared in the dark night sky.   **(1 mark)**

    b. We left our towels on the beach.   **(1 mark)**

    c. The soldiers fire at the practice target.   **(1 mark)**

    d. The aim of the game is to aim high.   **(1 mark)**

    e. Somehow we always manage to forget someone!   **(1 mark)**

    f. When you have finished, start the next task.   **(1 mark)**

Verb tenses

❶ Complete the following verb tense table.   **(7 marks)**

Simple Present	Simple Past
I decide	I decided
he eats	....
....	she was
they know	....
....	we went
you admit	....
you catch	....
....	we bought

❷ Rewrite the verb in brackets in each sentence so that it is in the **past progressive** tense. The first one has been done for you.

    a. Last Sunday, as we (**played**) *were playing* tennis, it started

    to pour down.

b. Our dog (**barked**) .... at the

strangers because he was nervous. **(1 mark)**

c. As I (**ate**) .... my breakfast, my

tooth fell out. **(1 mark)**

d. This morning, when we (**walked**) ....

to school, I saw my best friend Anna. **(1 mark)**

3 Underline the verb in the **present perfect** tense in each sentence below.

a. Mum has phoned the doctor for an appointment. **(1 mark)**

b. The sun has shone each day of our holiday. **(1 mark)**

c. Dad has had a toothache all weekend but he is feeling better now. **(1 mark)**

4 Rewrite the sentences below so that they are in the **present perfect** tense.

a. I wrote an invitation to Ushma, my best friend. **(1 mark)**

....

b. We saw the new Harry Potter film three times. **(1 mark)**

....

5 Rewrite the sentences below so that they are in the **past perfect** tense.

a. Mum baked a cake as a special surprise. **(1 mark)**

....

b. Our teacher organised a picnic for the last day of term. **(1 mark)**

....

Total $\frac{}{23}$

Modals indicating degrees of possibility

1 Circle **two modal verbs** indicating **possibility** in each of these sentences.

a. We may be going away next week but Dad may not be able to come. **(1 mark)**

b. Jon may play football this Saturday and if he does, he could be made team captain. **(1 mark)**

c. There can be as many as fifty children in the pool at any given time; there could even be more. **(1 mark)**

d. Joseph thought there might be heavy traffic so he asked if he could walk to school. **(1 mark)**

2 Insert appropriate modal verbs in these sentences.

a. I .... go to the shops later; I haven't made my mind up yet. **(1 mark)**

b. If the weather stays uncertain, we .... need to bring our waterproofs. **(1 mark)**

c. It .... not be possible to change our plans about going to the cinema. **(1 mark)**

d. It .... snow later according to the weather forecast. **(1 mark)**

3 Which sentence below shows that you are **most likely** to go to the cinema? Tick one. **(1 mark)**

I might go to the cinema tomorrow. ☐

I shall go to the cinema tomorrow. ☐

I may go to the cinema tomorrow. ☐

I could go to the cinema tomorrow. ☐

Adverbs indicating degrees of possibility

❶ Underline one adverb in each sentence that indicates **certainty** or **uncertainty**.

   a. We clearly aren't going to get there on time with this heavy traffic.   **(1 mark)**

   b. It's obviously the rush hour since it's 5 o'clock.   **(1 mark)**

   c. I certainly won't be coming at this time again.   **(1 mark)**

   d. Maybe we should have taken the country roads.   **(1 mark)**

❷ Insert an appropriate adverb in each sentence to indicate certainty.

   a. You .... have to eat more healthily.   **(1 mark)**

   b. Sarim .... isn't going to come now.   **(1 mark)**

   c. The shop is .... closed at this time of night.   **(1 mark)**

   d. Erin .... has more homework to finish.   **(1 mark)**

❸ Tick the correct box to indicate which adverbs in the paragraph below indicate **uncertainty** or **certainty**.   **(5 marks)**

> We **probably** won't be moving house before the summer. The builders might have difficulties finding the bricks we want and will **possibly** have to import them from abroad. It's **definitely** been a difficult time for Mum and Dad who **clearly** wanted us to be in well before the start of the school year. They've not had a minute to themselves and **perhaps** they will think twice about such a big project in the future.

Adverb	Certainty	Uncertainty
probably		
possibly		
definitely		
clearly		
perhaps		

Total —— 22

Adjectives

1 Underline **two adjectives** in each sentence.

a. Freddy, that naughty boy in Year 2, was in
   big trouble yet again.   **(1 mark)**

b. With his new football in his hands, Archie headed
   towards the muddy field.   **(1 mark)**

c. Although Brogan was nervous about the test, he was
   nonetheless a determined boy.   **(1 mark)**

d. Despite the atrocious weather conditions, the well-known
   team of explorers set off.   **(1 mark)**

2 Rewrite these sentences to make them more interesting by
   adding **one adjective** to describe **each noun**.

a. The cat slept on the mat.   **(1 mark)**

   ....

   ....

b. My sister came in and sat on the armchair.   **(1 mark)**

   ....

   ....

c. My mum cooked our dinner.   **(1 mark)**

   ....

   ....

d. We came across a field full of flowers.   **(1 mark)**

   ....

   ....

Adjectives comparing two nouns

1 Turn the words in brackets into **adjectives that show a comparison** between the two nouns in each sentence.

a. Matt is (old) than Thomas. **(1 mark)**

....

b. Freya's hair is (curly) than her big sister's. **(1 mark)**

....

c. I think the countryside is (beautiful) than inner-city areas. **(1 mark)**

....

d. Our homework was (interesting) this week than last week. **(1 mark)**

....

Adjectives comparing more than two nouns

1 Turn the words in brackets into suitable **adjectives that compare the subjects** in each sentence with everyone or everything else.

a. Mia had the (long) hair of all the girls in her class. **(1 mark)**

....

b. That actress had to be the (fascinating) person I'd ever interviewed. **(1 mark)**

....

c. We had the (intelligent) people on our quiz team. **(1 mark)**

....

d. It was the (disgusting) meal we'd ever eaten. **(1 mark)**

....

Total ——
16

Conjunctions that join two clauses of equal importance

1 Underline the **coordinating conjunction** in each of the following sentences.

    a. My mother likes to go to Spain on holiday but my father prefers France. **(1 mark)**

    b. We couldn't make swimming tonight for our car wouldn't start. **(1 mark)**

    c. I find long division really easy yet I struggle with long multiplication. **(1 mark)**

    d. It was way past our bedtime so our parents sent us to bed. **(1 mark)**

    e. We grabbed our swimsuits and set off for the swimming pool. **(1 mark)**

    f. Kathy hadn't a clue where the map was, nor did she really care. **(1 mark)**

2 Link the following sentences together with an appropriate coordinating conjunction. You might need to replace nouns with pronouns.

    a. Milo has a dog. Milo hasn't got a cat. **(1 mark)**

    ....

    b. Seb likes carrots. Seb likes cabbage. **(1 mark)**

    ....

    c. My sister is extremely tall. I am exceptionally short. **(1 mark)**

    ....

    d. Millie is amazing at tennis. She struggles with badminton. **(1 mark)**

    ....

    e. The rain was very heavy. The children couldn't play football. **(1 mark)**

    ....

Conjunctions that join a main clause to a subordinate clause

1 Circle or underline the **subordinating conjunctions** that join a main clause to a **subordinate clause** in the following sentences.

a. Although it was snowing very heavily, we managed to make it to school. **(1 mark)**

b. We had a very enjoyable trip to the cinema after we had eaten a tasty meal of pizza and salad. **(1 mark)**

c. Nick was passionate about football, though he had never been to a big match. **(1 mark)**

d. Sarah said we should meet at the shops since it was the easiest option. **(1 mark)**

e. Let's go swimming in the morning, unless you have something better to do. **(1 mark)**

2 Tick the correct box to indicate whether the words in bold are main clauses or subordinate clauses. **(4 marks)**

Sentence	Main clause	Subordinate clause
Even though there was a poor turn-out, the performers had a great night.		
Once the children knew the method, **they could solve the word problems**.		
We all rushed down to the shore, although it looked less inviting in the drizzle.		
As the sun began to set, a few people ventured out into the cooler air.		

3 **Tick** the sentence which is grammatically **incorrect**. **(1 mark)**

a. When he saw the size of the wolf, Hassan screamed in terror. ☐

b. There's no point having breakfast now because it's almost lunchtime. ☐

c. As Stella looked out across the sea to the distant horizon. ☐

d. In the middle of the night, as all went quiet, I heard a wolf howl. ☐

Total $\frac{}{21}$

1 Underline two **pronouns** in each sentence below.

    a. Katie and I unwrapped the sandwich, then quickly ate it. **(1 mark)**

    b. They brought Liam to see us last night. **(1 mark)**

    c. After Miles had picked some flowers, he put them
    in the kitchen. **(1 mark)**

    d. Sipping the smoothie slowly, she was sure it tasted
    rather odd. **(1 mark)**

2 Rewrite the following paragraph, inserting pronouns where they could replace nouns. **(4 marks)**

Sian and Chloe went to visit their grandma. Their grandma lived in an old, rambling manor by the seaside, covered in twisting ivy and with a front door hanging off its hinges. Approaching the front window, the girls knocked on the front window when they saw Grandma through the murky glass. When Grandma saw the girls Grandma was thrilled and ran outside to hug the girls. Grandma hadn't seen Sian and Chloe for a long time and Grandma asked if the girls would stay a while to help fix up the house and give the house a good clean.

....

....

....

....

....

....

....

Top tip!

Relative pronouns **refer back** to a noun.

3 Tick the correct box to indicate which sentence contains a **relative pronoun**.   (1 mark)

a. How many people living in the countryside do you know? ☐

b. We are all fairly sure that our homework is due in today. ☐

c. One of my relatives, who lives by the sea, is moving to the city. ☐

d. I'm not really very hungry, although I could manage a sandwich. ☐

4 Complete these sentences with a relative pronoun.

a. The lady, ... lived in the old cottage, moved
to a new house.   (1 mark)

b. The dog, ... owner was quite poorly, was very sad.   (1 mark)

c. We had all eaten the vegetable pie, ...
tasted amazing!   (1 mark)

d. There are lots of books .... I still haven't read yet.   (1 mark)

5 Underline the **possessive pronouns** in the following sentences.

a. I've got all my books but I can't find yours.   (1 mark)

b. Becca said the football was hers but Sam was sure it was his.   (1 mark)

c. Mum said they were their towels but I knew they were ours.   (1 mark)

d. I thought we were all going to my house but I'm happy to go to yours.   (1 mark)

6 Tick the correct box to indicate the type of **pronouns** in bold in
each sentence.   (2 marks)

Sentence	Possessive	Relative
These shoes are similar to **mine**.		
I have a baby brother **who** is more annoying than yours!		

Total —
19

Adverbs and adverbials

① Say whether the **adverbs** or **adverbials** in bold in these sentences show **how**, **where**, **when** or **how often**.

a. **After a while**, I went home as I had waited **patiently** for one hour. **(1 mark)**

   After a while: ....

   patiently: ....

b. **Cautiously**, I crept bit by bit **into the dark depths** of the gaping cave. **(1 mark)**

   Cautiously: ....

   into the dark depths: ....

c. **Still** feeling unconfident, Grace **reluctantly** tried the Maths questions. **(1 mark)**

   Still: ....

   reluctantly: ....

d. Inching **nervously** forward, the children **frequently** slipped on the ice. **(1 mark)**

   nervously: ....

   frequently: ....

② Insert an appropriate adverb to say more about the **verbs** in these sentences.

a. Far out to sea, the armada of ships moved .... across the horizon. **(1 mark)**

b. Having just won the final, the team jumped .... in the air. **(1 mark)**

c. ...., the bank robber was not charged, despite so many witnesses. **(1 mark)**

d. The children were all .... keen to finish their art. **(1 mark)**

Adverbs describing adjectives

❶ Underline the adverbs that say more about the **adjectives** in the following sentences.

a. Freddy said the day was completely ruined due to the bad weather. **(1 mark)**

b. All the children agreed that the fair had been really exciting. **(1 mark)**

c. Our summer holiday was quite disappointing as there wasn't a lot to do. **(1 mark)**

d. Our very naughty dog was in trouble for chewing Mum's slippers. **(1 mark)**

Fronted adverbials

❶ Which **two** sentences use a **fronted adverbial**? Tick two boxes. **(2 marks)**

a. In the far distance, Claire could see a boat sailing on the horizon. ☐

b. The old man, who only yesterday had been very ill, made a full recovery. ☐

c. Late last night, we heard heavy footsteps as we walked through the graveyard. ☐

d. Lucky old Ben, Cara thought, as she waved her friend off to the seaside. ☐

e. The Head Teacher was liked and respected by all the children. ☐

Adverbs giving more information about other adverbs

❶ Insert **quite**, **very**, **so**, **really** or **rather** before the **adverbs** in these sentences to make them more precise. You can use each word more than once.

a. Sarah skipped .... quickly to the shore's edge. **(1 mark)**

b. I was .... terribly excited at the news I almost burst. **(1 mark)**

c. I screamed when Dan .... nearly lost his footing. **(1 mark)**

d. After my little sister ate .... too much chocolate, she felt sick. **(1 mark)**

e. My brother was .... desperately afraid of the dark. **(1 mark)**

f. As it had started to rain, we went home .... willingly. **(1 mark)**

g. With most members of staff ill, the Head Teacher .... reluctantly closed the school. **(1 mark)**

Total — 21

1 Highlight the two **prepositions** that show **place** or **direction** in each sentence.

a. Zac hid behind the settee while his sister Sophie sat in the chair. **(1 mark)**

b. Mum found James's socks under the bed, inside his school shoes. **(1 mark)**

c. Monty the dog chased Tabitha the cat round the corner and up the tree. **(1 mark)**

d. We jumped quickly off the wall and hid beneath the oak tree. **(1 mark)**

e. We could make out a spider on the ceiling, crawling away from its web. **(1 mark)**

f. Sam liked to put lettuce in his sandwich before wrapping it in foil. **(1 mark)**

2 Tick the box against the sentence that contains a preposition in a phrase indicating **time**. **(1 mark)**

a. On Tuesdays, we go swimming with our friends. ☐

b. The leaves are starting to fall off the trees. ☐

c. Lee and Michael wanted to go to Australia to see kangaroos. ☐

d. The books were piled so high that they were going to topple. ☐

3 Complete the sentences with **prepositions**.

a. My family and I are travelling .... Cornwall

.... train. **(1 mark)**

b. High .... the mountain, the sun shone fiercely

.... the clear blue sky. **(1 mark)**

c. Grace and Chloe lifted Benji .... the

garden gate and .... the grass.   **(1 mark)**

d. When I got .... the bus, I put

my bag .... my seat.   **(1 mark)**

4 Write a preposition that can be used with each word.

a. similar ....   **(1 mark)**

b. according ....   **(1 mark)**

c. inspired ....   **(1 mark)**

d. equal ....   **(1 mark)**

e. complain ....   **(1 mark)**

f. interfere ....   **(1 mark)**

g. agree ....   **(1 mark)**

h. rely ....   **(1 mark)**

5 Which pair of prepositions is most suitable for this sentence? Tick one box.

The thief escaped by climbing .... a window and .... a getaway car.   **(1 mark)**

a. into / on

b. onto / through

c. through / into

d. behind / onto

Total $\frac{}{20}$

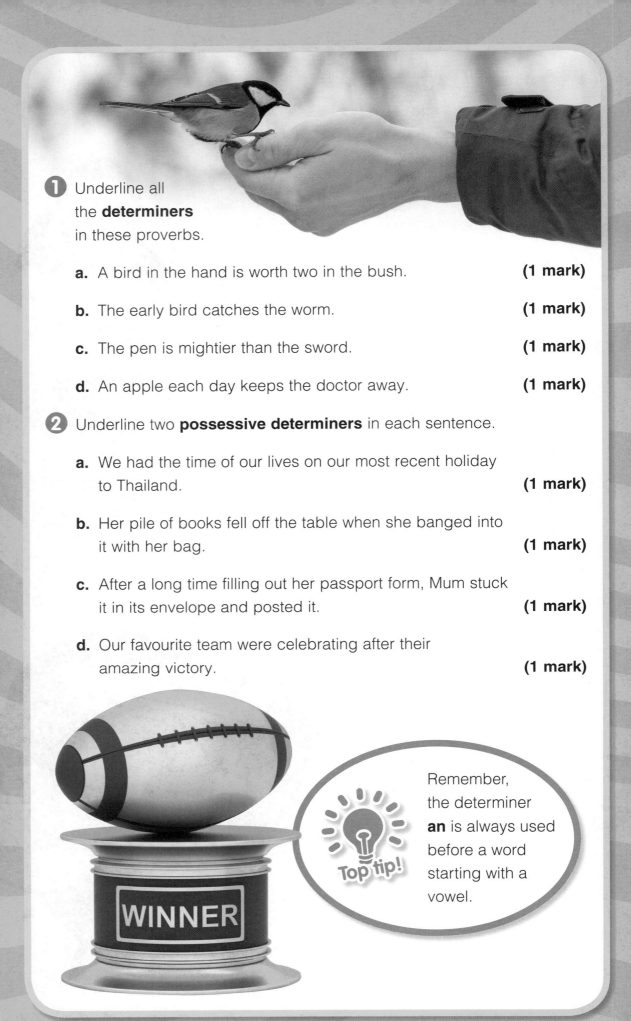

① Underline all the **determiners** in these proverbs.

   a. A bird in the hand is worth two in the bush.   **(1 mark)**

   b. The early bird catches the worm.   **(1 mark)**

   c. The pen is mightier than the sword.   **(1 mark)**

   d. An apple each day keeps the doctor away.   **(1 mark)**

② Underline two **possessive determiners** in each sentence.

   a. We had the time of our lives on our most recent holiday to Thailand.   **(1 mark)**

   b. Her pile of books fell off the table when she banged into it with her bag.   **(1 mark)**

   c. After a long time filling out her passport form, Mum stuck it in its envelope and posted it.   **(1 mark)**

   d. Our favourite team were celebrating after their amazing victory.   **(1 mark)**

Top tip!

Remember, the determiner **an** is always used before a word starting with a vowel.

3 Insert an appropriate **possessive determiner** in each of the following sentences.

a. We chatted for hours about .... excellent trip. **(1 mark)**

b. After .... stressful afternoon, we finally sorted it out. **(1 mark)**

c. Max put on .... orange t-shirt before going out to play. **(1 mark)**

d. They had a great time on .... holiday. **(1 mark)**

4 Insert the correct **possessive pronoun** in each of the following sentences.

a. That barking dog belongs to my neighbours. That dog is ....

(1 mark)

b. These books belong to my brother. These books are ....

(1 mark)

c. Those flowers were picked by Mum. Those flowers are ....

(1 mark)

d. We bought the pizza. The pizza is .... **(1 mark)**

Total 16

1 Give the definition of a **clause**. **(1 mark)**

....

2 Tick the box to show whether the words in bold are **clauses** or **phrases**. **(4 marks)**

Sentence	Phrase	Clause
We all breathed **a sigh of relief** when Kir put the ball in the net.		
Full of mischief, **the tiny puppy made his way over to the washing basket**.		
Everyone clapped in delight for the winning team.		
Talia stared **in wonder** at the sight of so much glittering treasure.		

3 Say whether the clauses in bold in these sentences are **main** or **subordinate**.

a. We all went off to the park **even though it was dreadful weather**. **(1 mark)**

....

b. **Jack was going skiing for the first time** and was feeling rather nervous. **(1 mark)**

....

c. **When he looked up from his breakfast**, Rob was shocked to see a dinosaur standing there! **(1 mark)**

....

d. Erin and Stella, **who had just been on an African safari**, were able to talk about lions and tigers. **(1 mark)**

....

e. **My walking boots**, which I had just cleaned, **were once again thick with mud**. **(1 mark)**

....

4 Join these pairs of sentences to make a **main clause** joined to a **subordinate clause** by a **conjunction**. An example has been done for you.

We went straight out to play.   We hadn't finished our meal.

We went straight out to play even though we hadn't finished our meal.

a. The fans cheered.   The red team won.   **(1 mark)**

....

b. The children lined up for assembly.   The fire-alarm started ringing.   **(1 mark)**

....

c. Stephanie didn't go to Eva's party.   She hadn't been invited.   **(1 mark)**

....

d. You should take the dog for a walk.   I took him out last time.   **(1 mark)**

....

e. I put the cat out in the garden.   It had stopped raining.   **(1 mark)**

....

Remember! A main clause makes sense on its own; a subordinate clause doesn't.

Top tip!

Total $\frac{}{15}$

Creating Sentences

1 Underline the **relative clauses** in the following sentences.

a. The old lady, who I met yesterday on the beach, has called round with flowers. **(1 mark)**

b. After our lunch we went to the cinema, which was in a nearby shopping complex. **(1 mark)**

c. Sarim and Sophie, whose parents were on holiday, stayed with us for the weekend. **(1 mark)**

d. My dad's car, which had only just been repaired, broke down on the motorway. **(1 mark)**

e. The pitch where we played our match was very muddy. **(1 mark)**

f. The bakery that we use is on the corner. **(1 mark)**

2 Circle the **incorrect relative pronoun** in these sentences. Write the correct relative pronoun in the answer space.

a. I thanked the old man next door which feeds my cat when we are away. **(1 mark)**

....

b. My sister that has just returned from her school trip has come home very tired and grumpy. **(1 mark)**

....

c. Our neighbour, who garden shed was broken into, reported it to the police. **(1 mark)**

....

d. Those books, who we've all read, can go to the charity shop. **(1 mark)**

....

3 Insert a suitable **relative pronoun** in the sentences below.

a. We have been lucky with the weather, ... was rather grim yesterday.

(1 mark)

b. The day .... my baby brother was born was the happiest day of my life!

(1 mark)

c. My best friend, ... is moving house next month, is packing up already.

(1 mark)

d. I can't believe that our supper, ... we put in the oven ages ago, still isn't ready!

(1 mark)

4 Rewrite these sentences using **relative pronouns**.
An example has been done for you.

Cerys's books, scattered untidily on the table, were all mystery stories.
Cerys's books, which were scattered untidily on the table, were all mystery stories.

a. My mum, a former Olympic swimming champion, took us to the local pool.

(1 mark)

....

b. Our school grounds, recently damaged in a flood, now look better than ever.

(1 mark)

....

c. Max, eager to win some medals, won the 100 metre race and the hurdles. **(1 mark)**

....

The relative pronoun **whose** can't be omitted.
For example:
The cat, whose owner was away, stayed at a neighbour's.

But others can be omitted:
The cat, who was sitting on the wall, purred softly.
The cat, sitting on the wall, purred softly.

Top tip!

Total $\frac{}{17}$

1 Write two examples of a **statement**.

a. .... **(1 mark)**

b. .... **(1 mark)**

2 Write two examples of a **question**.

a. .... **(1 mark)**

b. .... **(1 mark)**

3 Write two examples of a **command**.

a. .... **(1 mark)**

b. .... **(1 mark)**

4 Write two examples of an **exclamation**, starting with 'How' or 'What'.

a. .... **(1 mark)**

b. .... **(1 mark)**

It makes sense that an exclamation mark comes at the end of an exclamation and a question mark at the end of a question! Often an exclamation mark comes at the end of a command too.

5 Use **command verbs** to complete these sentences.

a. .... your breakfast immediately! **(1 mark)**

b. .... at the pedestrian crossing and

.... both ways before you cross. **(1 mark)**

c. .... your homework then

.... it to your teacher. **(1 mark)**

d. .... a thank-you note to your friends
who bought you presents. **(1 mark)**

6 Tick the correct box to indicate the sentence type.　　　　**(4 marks)**

Sentence	Statement	Question	Command	Exclamation
Take the first road on the left, then turn left.				
How many more days until the holidays?				
What massive teeth that crocodile has!				
It's a perfect day for a picnic.				

7 Write questions that would match these answers.

a. ....

.... **(1 mark)**

There are approximately 250 children, aged 4–11.

b. ....

.... **(1 mark)**

We went to Europe for two weeks and had a weekend in Scotland.

c. ....

.... **(1 mark)**

Turn right at the end of the road, then first left after the post office.

1 Underline the **subjects** of the following sentences.

   a. Finn watched the netball match. **(1 mark)**

   b. Last week, my friends and I took the bus home. **(1 mark)**

   c. After a while, Sasha stopped talking and listened to the teacher. **(1 mark)**

   d. The rain lashed continuously all through the night. **(1 mark)**

   e. Whenever we can, my sisters and I help our mum with the washing-up. **(1 mark)**

   f. You have eaten all the chocolates! **(1 mark)**

2 Tick the sentence where the verb **does not agree** with the subject. Then write the sentence correctly in the space. **(1 mark)**

   a. My parents aren't always in agreement about how long I should spend on homework. ☐

   b. Aisha and Will doesn't have packed lunches with them today. ☐

   c. The herd of elephants is charging swiftly through the jungle. ☐

   d. Saskia and I are in trouble for not listening more carefully. ☐

....

3 Rewrite the following sentences in the **simple past** tense.

   a. I am hungry. **(1 mark)**

....

   b. She is ten years old. **(1 mark)**

....

   c. They are sad. **(1 mark)**

....

d. They go to bed early. **(1 mark)**

....

e. She goes to school on the bus. **(1 mark)**

....

f. I go swimming every day. **(1 mark)**

....

4 Rewrite each sentence so that the subject agrees with the verb in the tense indicated.

a. We walks towards the cliff edge and takes care that the wind didn't blow
our hats off. **(1 mark)**

Simple past: ....

....

b. As you discovers, the water were very deep in the harbour. **(1 mark)**

Simple past: ....

....

c. She take great care when she draw diagrams. **(1 mark)**

Simple past: ....

d. At 6 o'clock in the morning, were it any wonder I were too tired to eat? **(1 mark)**

Simple present: ....

....

e. Sol run over the finish line then throw himself on the ground in relief. **(1 mark)**

Simple present: ....

....

f. We often watches animated films on TV but they is much better at the cinema. **(1 mark)**

Simple present: ....

....

Total $\frac{}{19}$

1 **Underline** the **subject** and **circle** the **object** in the following sentences.

a. My parents love watching the football. **(1 mark)**

b. A wasp has just stung me. **(1 mark)**

c. The three children pushed the garden gate. **(1 mark)**

d. The policeman arrested the thief. **(1 mark)**

e. The horses were eating hay. **(1 mark)**

f. My meddling little brother has broken my computer. **(1 mark)**

2 Write sentences containing an appropriate subject and object for these verbs.

a. to eat **(1 mark)**

....

b. to carry **(1 mark)**

....

c. to bite **(1 mark)**

....

d. to marry **(1 mark)**

....

e to play **(1 mark)**

....

f. to read **(1 mark)**

....

3 Which sentence below does not contain an object? Tick one box.   **(1 mark)**

   a. There are ten girls skipping. ☐

   b. We are eating our supper. ☐

   c. John likes strawberries. ☐

   d. I've just read the books on that shelf. ☐

4 Add an object to expand these simple sentences.
An example has been done for you.

The choir sang very well.
The choir sang the songs very well.

   a. My mum likes baking.   **(1 mark)**

   ....

   b. Do you like drawing?   **(1 mark)**

   ....

   c. My sister is great at riding.   **(1 mark)**

   ....

   d. We've all been playing.   **(1 mark)**

   ....

Top tip!

Remember to look at the verb in a sentence then ask the question, **what or who is it acting on?** The answer will tell you what the object is, if there is one.

Total $\frac{}{17}$

1 Write two sentences in the **active voice**.

a. .... **(1 mark)**

b. .... **(1 mark)**

2 Write two sentences in the **passive voice**.

a. .... **(1 mark)**

b. .... **(1 mark)**

3 Turn these sentences from the **active** to the **passive voice**.

a. The children's parents took them to the disco for
the Year 6 treat. **(1 mark)**

....

....

b. Sir Edmund Hillary and Sherpa Tenzing conquered
Everest in 1953. **(1 mark)**

....

....

c. The cooks burned the apple pie because the oven
was too hot. **(1 mark)**

....

....

d. When the bin started to overflow, Millie threw out
the rubbish. **(1 mark)**

....

....

e. The dentist extracted my big sister's tooth. **(1 mark)**

....

....

f. Finally, the determined junior team won the
Champion's Cup. **(1 mark)**

....

....

4 Tick the correct box to show whether the following sentences are in the **active voice**
or the **passive voice**.

Sentence	Active voice	Passive voice
The angry wasps stung the children.		
My mother brought my friends and me to the cinema.		
A family was rescued from the blaze by a fireman.		
We were given an ultimatum by our teacher.		
The thieves were being pursued.		
We left our picnic blanket by the edge of the river.		

(6 marks)

5 Turn these sentences from the passive voice into the active voice.

a. My energetic dog was walked all week by an enthusiastic dog-walker. **(1 mark)**

....

....

b. The transatlantic race was completed by the team in record time. **(1 mark)**

....

....

c. Three phone calls were received by the emergency team last night. **(1 mark)**

....

....

d. The newspaper article written by the young journalist was fascinating. **(1 mark)**

....

....

Total $\frac{}{20}$

1 Underline the **direct speech** in the following passage. **(3 marks)**

When Benji heard the thunder in the middle of the night, he said it

was the loudest noise he'd ever heard. "Make it go away!" he shouted.

His mum said that it couldn't hurt him and it might help to count the

seconds between the thunder claps and the lightning bolts.

"It's nature, sweetheart, and it won't last forever," she reassured him.

"Come on, let's count together."

"One, two, three, four...," they counted. By eight, Benji was

already asleep.

2 The following sentences are examples of direct speech but all the punctuation has been left out.

Rewrite the sentences and insert **all** the missing punctuation in the correct places.
An example has been done for you.

We really should visit Grandma this afternoon said Mum
"We really should visit Grandma this afternoon," said Mum.

a. I would really like to go to the cinema to see that new
Spiderman film Paul said **(1 mark)**

....

....

b. We knew that eventually we would move to America the
children told their neighbours **(1 mark)**

....

....

....

Top tip!

Use a range of different words for **said** to make your writing more interesting.

c. Start running now Jack screamed **(1 mark)**

....

d. Taylor said I hope I remembered to put the chocolate brownies
in the picnic basket **(1 mark)**

....

....

e. Have you brought your library book in today asked the librarian **(1 mark)**

....

③ Rewrite these sentences using inverted commas to show direct speech. Change the
other punctuation if necessary.

a. Max asked Billy if he would play football with him. **(1 mark)**

....

b. Harry announced that everyone could come to his house for tea. **(1 mark)**

....

c. All the Year 6 spectators shouted to the lacrosse team to score. **(1 mark)**

....

d. Honor asked her teacher if she could have some extra time in the
reading test. **(1 mark)**

....

④ How many words to replace **said** when using direct speech can
you think of? Write them below. **(up to 10 marks)**

....	....	....	....	....
....	....	....	....	....

Top tip! Vary your writing by using
a mixture of direct speech
and reported speech.

Total — 22

1 a. Give some differences between **informal** and **formal** speech and writing. **(2 marks)**

....

....

b. When might you use each type? ....

.... **(2 marks)**

2 Would you use **informal** or **formal** writing for the following?

a. A text to your friend. .... **(1 mark)**

b. A letter to the Head Teacher. .... **(1 mark)**

c. A postcard to your mum and dad. .... **(1 mark)**

d. A letter to an author whose book you liked. .... **(1 mark)**

e. Your diary. .... **(1 mark)**

f. An email to your close friends. .... **(1 mark)**

g. Your speech for a public speaking competition.

.... **(1 mark)**

3 Write two diary entries for a recent weekend, using the appropriate type of language for this genre. **(4 marks)**

Saturday
....
....
....
....

Sunday
....
....
....
....

4 Insert the **subjunctive** form of the verb **to be** to complete these sentences. **(2 marks)**

a. Her Majesty requires that all visitors .... respectful of the palace grounds.

b. If only we .... able to join you on holiday!

5 You are introducing your favourite author in assembly who is visiting your school to talk about his / her book.
Write a short speech welcoming him / her and giving some background information about them and their latest book. **(4 marks)**

....

....

....

....

....

....

....

6 Rewrite the following sentences using **Standard English**.

a. We ain't gonna go to the park 'coz we's got visitors. **(1 mark)**

....

b. Pick them books up now else I'll be proper cross. **(1 mark)**

....

c. She would of helped youse if youse would of asked. **(1 mark)**

....

d. I don't want no chips with me chicken. **(1 mark)**

....

....

Total $\frac{}{25}$

1 Why do we use **punctuation marks**? ....

.... **(1 mark)**

2 When do we use **capital letters** and **full stops**? ....

.... **(1 mark)**

3 Insert **capital letters** and **full stops** into the following passage
so that it makes sense. **(4 marks)**

when maggie and jack reached the outskirts of london, they were quite overwhelmed at the sight of some of the iconic buildings looming before them were the houses of parliament, then big ben, next westminster abbey and st paul's cathedral taking a boat on the river thames, the children were wide-eyed in awe and amazement as they saw the city from a different perspective all they could think about was how impressed their teacher, mrs muggins, would be when they went in to school on monday morning

4 Only one of the sentences below is correctly punctuated.
Tick the box to indicate which one. **(1 mark)**

Sentence	Correct?
My brother said his friend pat was going to watch the new harry potter film with him.	
At breezybank primary school, the best teachers, in my opinion, are mrs mason and mr burns.	
after a long wait in London, the children got on the bus to Cambridge and went home.	
My next adventure will be to take a raft down the River Ganges in India.	
Every wednesday, I go to the swimming baths with Claire and Sam.	

Top tip! Capital letters are not joined to the next letter – they stand alone and should be twice the height of short letters such as **a** or **o**.

Capital letters and full stops

5 Rewrite the following sentences, correcting any missing or wrongly placed **capital letters** and **full stops**.

a. "I'm off to the Shops. now," said bill to his Sister. "there's a special Discount on at sweetsavers" **(1 mark)**

....

....

b. we couldn't understand how maddie had forgotten her Homework for the second time in a Week our teacher had told her many Times **(1 mark)**

....

....

c. looking out of the window tom was struggling. to see his dad's volvo through the. fog then it started to clear and before he knew it tom was outside playing. in the Sunshine **(1 mark)**

....

....

d. megan and amy were off to paris. to visit the eiffel tower, which they hoped to climb to the Top they were going with their Cousin arthur who speaks french fluently **(1 mark)**

....

....

e. i watched the lion king when we went to London it was truly amazing and probably the best performance I've ever seen I would actually go back and watch it again **(1 mark)**

....

....

When I write, I remember to make capital letters tall. I do not join them.

Total $\frac{}{12}$

1 When do we use **question marks**? **(1 mark)**

....

2 When do we use **exclamation marks**? **(1 mark)**

....

3 Add either a **question mark** or an **exclamation mark** to these sentences.

a. What dreadful weather it was.......... **(1 mark)**

b. "I'm going home now, aren't you.........." **(1 mark)**

c. "There's not much point in staying any longer, is there.........." **(1 mark)**

d. How shocked we were to hear about the floods.......... **(1 mark)**

e. Had they really arrived that morning in glorious sunshine..........

(1 mark)

4 Write suitable questions for these answers.

a. .... **(1 mark)**

He had white hair, round glasses and was a little stooped.

b. .... **(1 mark)**

Three girls, two boys and a small, yappy dog.

c. .... **(1 mark)**

I cooked it according to the recipe.

d. .... **(1 mark)**

Every day of the week except Sundays.

GRAMMAR TERMS

Nouns
pages 4–5
Nouns

1 a. We ate the <u>pizza</u> and drank our <u>juice</u>.
(1 mark)

b. She swapped her <u>book</u> at the <u>library</u>.
(1 mark)

c. He dropped lots of <u>pencils</u> on the <u>floor</u>.
(1 mark)

d. The <u>girls</u> stopped talking and listened to their <u>teacher</u>. **(1 mark)**

e. Our <u>school</u> closed early because of the heavy <u>snow</u>. **(1 mark)**

f. <u>Scarves</u>, <u>gloves</u> and <u>hats</u> – all were packed for the <u>trip</u>. **(1 mark)**

Noun types

1 They either start with a capital letter because they are at the beginning of the sentence or they are proper nouns. **(1 mark)**

2 a. The <u>ducks</u> wandered down the <u>road</u> and into the <u>field</u>. **(1 mark)**

b. Our <u>team</u> finished early on <u>Wednesday</u> because of the <u>snow</u>. **(1 mark)**

c. <u>Phil</u> showed great <u>courage</u> when faced with the <u>tiger</u>. **(1 mark)**

d. <u>Prince William</u> visited <u>Wales</u> at the <u>beginning</u> of <u>July</u>. **(1 mark)**

e. My <u>football</u> hit the top <u>bar</u> of the <u>net</u>. **(1 mark)**

f. We went in the <u>sea</u>, although the <u>weather</u> was grim and the <u>waves</u> rough. **(1 mark)**

Expanded noun phrases

1 a. <u>The beautiful blue butterfly</u> landed on <u>my bare shoulder</u>. **(1 mark)**

b. We showed <u>a lot of courage</u> in spite of <u>the awful danger</u> we were in. **(1 mark)**

c. <u>My old grandfather</u> kept <u>two herds of cows</u> on <u>his five-acre farm</u>. **(1 mark)**

d. <u>Our local primary school</u> has <u>a well-stocked library</u> full of <u>interesting books</u>. **(1 mark)**

e. Sasha went to <u>the beautiful islands</u> of Guernsey and Jersey for <u>his first-ever holiday</u>. **(1 mark)**

f. After eating <u>cheese and ham sandwiches</u>, <u>my little sister</u> and I headed home. **(1 mark)**

2 Answers will vary. Examples:

countryside	The never-ending countryside
determination	His relentless determination
disgust	My utter disgust
ocean	The vast ocean
swarm	A dense swarm of bees

(5 marks)

Verbs
pages 6–7
Identifying verbs

1 a. The fire <u>roared</u> in the dark night sky.
(1 mark)

b. We <u>left</u> our towels on the beach.
(1 mark)

c. The soldiers <u>fire</u> at the practice target.
(1 mark)

d. The aim of the game <u>is</u> <u>to aim</u> high.
(1 mark)

e. Somehow we always <u>manage to forget</u> someone! **(1 mark)**

f. When you <u>have finished</u>, <u>start</u> the next task. **(1 mark)**

Verb tenses

1

Simple Present	Simple Past
I decide	I decided
he eats	**he ate**
she is	she was
they know	**they knew**
we go	we went
you admit	**you admitted**
you catch	**you caught**
we buy	we bought

(7 marks)

2 b. Our dog **was barking** at the strangers because he was nervous. **(1 mark)**

c. As I **was eating** my breakfast, my tooth fell out. **(1 mark)**

d. This morning, when we **were walking** to school, I saw my best friend Anna. **(1 mark)**

3 a. Mum <u>has phoned</u> the doctor for an appointment. **(1 mark)**

b. The sun <u>has shone</u> each day of our holiday. **(1 mark)**

c. Dad <u>has had</u> a toothache all weekend but he is feeling better now. **(1 mark)**

4 a. I **have written** an invitation to Ushma, my best friend. **(1 mark)**

b. We **have seen** the new Harry Potter film three times. **(1 mark)**

5 a. Mum **had baked** a cake as a special surprise. **(1 mark)**

b. Our teacher **had organised** a picnic for the last day of term. **(1 mark)**

Modal verbs
pages 8–9
Modals indicating degrees of possibility

1 a. We (may) be going away next week but there's a chance Dad (may) not be able to come. **(1 mark)**

b. Jon (may) play football this Saturday and if he does, he (could) be made team captain. **(1 mark)**

c. There (can) be as many as fifty children in the pool at any given time; there (could) even be more **(1 mark)**

d. Joseph thought there (might) be heavy traffic so he asked if he (could) walk to school. **(1 mark)**

2 Answers may vary. Examples:

a. I may go to the shops later; I haven't made my mind up yet. **(1 mark)**

b. If the weather stays uncertain, we may need to bring our waterproofs. **(1 mark)**

c. It may not be possible to change our plans about going to the cinema. **(1 mark)**

d. It might snow later according to the weather forecast. **(1 mark)**

3 I shall go to the cinema tomorrow. ✓ **(1 mark)**

Adverbs indicating degrees of possibility

1 a. We clearly aren't going to get there on time with this heavy traffic. **(1 mark)**

b. It's obviously the rush hour since it's 5 o'clock. **(1 mark)**

c. I certainly won't be coming at this time again. **(1 mark)**

d. Maybe we should have taken the country roads. **(1 mark)**

2 Answers will vary. Examples:

a. You definitely have to eat more healthily. **(1 mark)**

b. Sarim obviously isn't going to come now. **(1 mark)**

c. The shop is surely closed at this time of night. **(1 mark)**

d. Erin clearly has more homework to finish. **(1 mark)**

3

Adverb	Certainty	Uncertainty
probably		✓
possibly		✓
definitely	✓	
clearly	✓	
perhaps		✓

(5 marks)

Adjectives
pages 10–11
Adjectives

1 a. Freddy, that naughty boy in Year 2, was in big trouble yet again. **(1 mark)**

b. With his new football in his hands, Archie headed towards the muddy field. **(1 mark)**

c. Although Brogan was nervous about the test, he was nonetheless a determined boy. **(1 mark)**

d. Despite the atrocious weather conditions, the well-known team of explorers set off. **(1 mark)**

2 Answers will vary. Examples:

a. The **furry** cat slept on the **grubby** mat. **(1 mark)**

b. My **annoying** sister came in and sat on the **comfiest** armchair. **(1 mark)**

c. My **wonderful** mum cooked our **favourite** dinner. **(1 mark)**

d. We came across a **vast** field full of **beautiful** flowers. **(1 mark)**

Adjectives comparing two nouns

1 a. Matt is older than Thomas. **(1 mark)**

b. Freya's hair is curlier than her big sister's. **(1 mark)**

c. I think the countryside is more / less beautiful than inner-city areas. **(1 mark)**

d. Our homework was more / less interesting this week than last week. **(1 mark)**

Adjectives comparing more than two nouns

1 a. Mia had the longest hair of all the girls in her class. **(1 mark)**

b. That actress had to be the most / least fascinating person I'd ever interviewed. **(1 mark)**

c. We had the most / least intelligent people on our quiz team. **(1 mark)**

d. It was the most disgusting meal we'd ever eaten. **(1 mark)**

Conjunctions

pages 12–13
Conjunctions that join two clauses of equal importance

1. **a.** My mother likes to go to Spain on holiday <u>but</u> my father prefers France. **(1 mark)**
   b. We couldn't make swimming tonight <u>for</u> our car wouldn't start. **(1 mark)**
   c. I find long division really easy <u>yet</u> I struggle with long multiplication. **(1 mark)**
   d. It was way past our bedtime <u>so</u> our parents sent us to bed. **(1 mark)**
   e. We grabbed our swimsuits <u>and</u> set off for the swimming pool. **(1 mark)**
   f. Kathy hadn't a clue where the map was, <u>nor</u> did she really care. **(1 mark)**

2. **a.** Milo has a dog <u>but</u> he hasn't got a cat. **(1 mark)**
   b. Seb likes carrots <u>and</u> he likes cabbage. **(1 mark)**
   c. My sister is extremely tall <u>but / yet</u> I am exceptionally short. **(1 mark)**
   d. Millie is amazing at tennis <u>but / yet</u> she struggles with badminton. **(1 mark)**
   e. The rain was very heavy <u>so</u> the children couldn't play football. **(1 mark)**

Conjunctions that join a main clause to a subordinate clause

1. **a.** <u>Although</u> it was snowing very heavily, we managed to make it to school. **(1 mark)**
   b. We had a very enjoyable trip to the cinema <u>after</u> we had eaten a tasty meal of pizza and salad. **(1 mark)**
   c. Nick was passionate about football, <u>though</u> he had never been to a big match. **(1 mark)**
   d. Sarah said we should meet at the shops <u>since</u> it was the easiest option. **(1 mark)**
   e. Let's go swimming in the morning, <u>unless</u> you have something better to do. **(1 mark)**

2.

Sentence	Main clause	Subordinate clause
Even though there was a poor turn-out, the performers had a great night.		✓
Once the children knew the method, **they could solve the word problems**.	✓	
We all rushed down to the shore, although it looked less inviting in the drizzle.	✓	
As the sun began to set, a few people ventured out into the cooler air.		✓

(4 marks)

3. **c.** As Stella looked out across the sea to the distant horizon. ☑ **(1 mark)**

Pronouns

pages 14–15

1. **a.** Katie and <u>I</u> unwrapped the sandwich, then quickly ate <u>it</u>. **(1 mark)**
   b. <u>They</u> brought Liam to see <u>us</u> last night. **(1 mark)**
   c. After Miles had picked some flowers, <u>he</u> put <u>them</u> in the kitchen. **(1 mark)**
   d. Sipping the smoothie slowly, <u>she</u> was sure <u>it</u> tasted rather odd. **(1 mark)**

2. Sian and Chloe went to visit their grandma. **She** lived in an old, rambling manor by the seaside, covered in twisting ivy and with a front door hanging off its hinges. Approaching the front window, the girls knocked on **it** when they saw Grandma through the murky glass. When **she** saw **them**, Grandma was thrilled and ran outside to hug **them**. **She** hadn't seen **them** for a long time and **she** asked if **they** would stay a while to help fix up the house and give **it** a good clean. **(4 marks)**

3. **c.** One of my relatives, who lives by the sea, is moving to the city. ☑ **(1 mark)**

4. **a.** The lady, <u>who</u> lived in the old cottage, moved to new house. **(1 mark)**
   b. The dog, <u>whose</u> owner was quite poorly, was very sad. **(1 mark)**
   c. We had all eaten the vegetable pie, <u>which</u> tasted amazing! **(1 mark)**
   d. There are lots of books <u>that/which</u> I still haven't read yet. **(1 mark)**

5. **a.** I've got all my books but I can't find <u>yours</u>. **(1 mark)**
   b. Becca said the football was <u>hers</u> but Sam was sure it was <u>his</u>. **(1 mark)**
   c. Mum said they were their towels but I knew they were <u>ours</u>. **(1 mark)**
   d. I thought we were all going to my house but I'm happy to go to <u>yours</u>. **(1 mark)**

6.

Sentence	Possessive	Relative
These shoes are similar to **mine**.	✓	
I have a baby brother **who** is more annoying than yours!		✓

(2 marks)

Adverbs and adverbials

pages 16–17
Adverbs and adverbials

1. **a.** After a while: <u>when</u>; patiently: <u>how</u> **(1 mark)**
   b. Cautiously: <u>how</u>; into the dark depths: <u>where</u> **(1 mark)**

c. Still: <u>when</u>; reluctantly: <u>how</u> **(1 mark)**

d. nervously: <u>how</u>; frequently: <u>how often</u> **(1 mark)**

2 Answers will vary. Examples:

a. Far out to sea, the armada of ships moved **elegantly/swiftly** across the horizon. **(1 mark)**

b. Having just won the final, the team jumped **joyfully/enthusiastically** in the air. **(1 mark)**

c. **Incredibly/unbelievably**, the bank robber was not charged, despite so many witnesses. **(1 mark)**

d. The children were all **desperately/ incredibly** keen to finish their art. **(1 mark)**

Adverbs describing adjectives

1 a. Freddy said the day was <u>completely</u> ruined due to the bad weather. **(1 mark)**

b. All the children agreed that the fair had been <u>really</u> exciting. **(1 mark)**

c. Our summer holiday was <u>quite</u> disappointing as there wasn't a lot to do. **(1 mark)**

d. Our <u>very</u> naughty dog was in trouble for chewing Mum's slippers. **(1 mark)**

Fronted adverbials

1 a. In the far distance, Claire could see a boat sailing on the horizon. ☑ **(1 mark)**

c. Late last night, we heard heavy footsteps as we walked through the graveyard. ☑ **(1 mark)**

Adverbs giving more information about other adverbs

1 a. Sarah skipped <u>quite/very/really/rather</u> quickly to the shore's edge. **(1 mark)**

b. I was <u>so</u> terribly excited at the news I almost burst. **(1 mark)**

c. I screamed when Dan <u>very/so</u> nearly lost his footing. **(1 mark)**

d. After my little sister ate <u>rather</u> too much chocolate she felt sick. **(1 mark)**

e. My brother was <u>quite/very/so/ really/rather</u> desperately afraid of the dark. **(1 mark)**

f. As it had started to rain, we went home <u>quite/really/very/rather</u> willingly. **(1 mark)**

g. With most members of staff ill, the Head Teacher <u>rather/really/very</u> reluctantly closed the school. **(1 mark)**

Prepositions

pages 18–19

1 a. Zac hid **behind** the settee while his sister Sophie sat **in** the chair. **(1 mark)**

b. Mum found James's socks **under** the bed **inside** his school shoes. **(1 mark)**

c. Monty the dog chased Tabitha the cat **round** the corner and **up** the tree. **(1 mark)**

d. We jumped quickly **off** the wall and hid **beneath** the oak tree. **(1 mark)**

e. We could make out a spider **on** the ceiling crawling away **from** its web. **(1 mark)**

f. Sam liked to put lettuce **in** his sandwich before wrapping it **in** foil. **(1 mark)**

2 a. On Tuesdays, we go swimming with our friends. ☑ **(1 mark)**

3 a. My family and I are travelling **to / around** Cornwall **by** train. **(1 mark)**

b. High **above** the mountain, the sun shone fiercely **in** the clear blue sky. **(1 mark)**

c. Grace and Chloe lifted Benji **over** the garden gate and **onto** the grass. **(1 mark)**

d. When I got **on** the bus, I put my bag **under / on** my seat. **(1 mark)**

4 a. similar <u>to</u> **(1 mark)**

b. according <u>to</u> **(1 mark)**

c. inspired <u>by/to</u> **(1 mark)**

d. equal <u>to</u> **(1 mark)**

e. complain <u>about/of</u> **(1 mark)**

f. interfere <u>with</u> **(1 mark)**

g. agree <u>with/to</u> **(1 mark)**

h. rely <u>on</u> **(1 mark)**

5 c. through / into ☑ **(1 mark)**

Determiners

pages 20–21

1 a. <u>A</u> bird in <u>the</u> hand is worth two in <u>the</u> bush. **(1 mark)**

b. <u>The</u> early bird catches <u>the</u> worm. **(1 mark)**

c. <u>The</u> pen is mightier than <u>the</u> sword. **(1 mark)**

d. <u>An</u> apple <u>each</u> day keeps <u>the</u> doctor away. **(1 mark)**

2 a. We had the time of <u>our</u> lives on <u>our</u> most recent holiday to Thailand. **(1 mark)**

b. <u>Her</u> pile of books fell off the table when she banged into it with <u>her</u> bag. **(1 mark)**

c. After a long time filling out <u>her</u> passport form, Mum stuck it in <u>its</u> envelope and posted it. **(1 mark)**

d. <u>Our</u> favourite team were celebrating after <u>their</u> amazing victory. **(1 mark)**

3 **a.** We chatted for hours about **our** excellent trip.

  (1 mark)

  b. After **my/their/our** stressful afternoon, we finally sorted it out.

  (1 mark)

  c. Max put on **his** orange t-shirt before going out to play.

  (1 mark)

  d. They had a great time on **their** holiday.

  (1 mark)

4 **a.** That dog is **theirs**.

  (1 mark)

  b. These books are **his**.

  (1 mark)

  c. Those flowers are **hers**.

  (1 mark)

  d. The pizza is **ours**.

  (1 mark)

CREATING SENTENCES

Phrases and clauses
pages 22–23

1 A clause contains a verb and can sometimes make sense as a sentence.

  (1 mark)

2

Sentence	Phrase	Clause
We all breathed **a sigh of relief** when Kir put the ball in the net.	✓	
Full of mischief, **the tiny puppy made his way over to the washing basket**.		✓
Everyone clapped in delight for the winning team.		✓
Talia stared **in wonder** at the sight of so much glittering treasure.	✓	

  (4 marks)

3 **a.** subordinate clause **(1 mark)**
  b. main clause **(1 mark)**
  c. subordinate clause **(1 mark)**
  d. subordinate clause **(1 mark)**
  e. main clause **(1 mark)**

4 Answers may vary. Examples:
  a. The fans cheered <u>after</u> the red team won. **(1 mark)**
  b. The children lined up for assembly <u>as</u> the fire-alarm started ringing. **(1 mark)**
  c. Stephanie didn't go to Eva's party <u>because/as</u> she hadn't been invited. **(1 mark)**
  d. You should take the dog for a walk <u>because/since</u> I took him out last time. **(1 mark)**
  e. I put the cat out in the garden <u>after/once</u> it had stopped raining. **(1 mark)**

Relative clauses
pages 24–25

1 **a.** The old lady, <u>who I met yesterday on the beach</u>, has called round with flowers. **(1 mark)**
  b. After our lunch we went to the cinema, <u>which was in a nearby shopping complex</u>. **(1 mark)**

  c. Sarim and Sophie, <u>whose parents were on holiday</u>, stayed with us for the weekend. **(1 mark)**
  d. My dad's car, <u>which had only just been repaired</u>, broke down on the motorway. **(1 mark)**
  e. The pitch <u>where we played our match</u> was very muddy. **(1 mark)**
  f. The bakery <u>that we use</u> is on the corner. **(1 mark)**

2 **a.** I thanked the old man next door <u>who</u> feeds my cat when we are away. **(1 mark)**
  b. My sister <u>who</u> has just returned from her school trip has come home very tired and grumpy. **(1 mark)**
  c. Our neighbour, <u>whose</u> garden shed was broken into, reported it to the police. **(1 mark)**
  d. Those books, <u>which</u> we've all read, can go to the charity shop. **(1 mark)**

3 **a.** We have been lucky with the weather, <u>which</u> was rather grim yesterday. **(1 mark)**
  b. The day <u>when/that</u> my baby brother was born was the happiest day of my life! **(1 mark)**
  c. My best friend, <u>who</u> is moving house next month, is packing up already. **(1 mark)**
  d. I can't believe that our supper, <u>which</u> we put in the oven ages ago, still isn't ready! **(1 mark)**

4 **a.** My mum, **who is** a former Olympic swimming champion, took us to the local pool. **(1 mark)**
  b. Our school grounds, **which were** recently damaged in a flood, now look better than ever.

  (1 mark)

  c. Max, **who was** eager to win some medals, won the 100 metre race and the hurdles. **(1 mark)**

Sentence types
pages 26–27

1 Accept any two appropriate statements. **(2 marks)**

2 Accept any two appropriate questions. **(2 marks)**

3 Accept any two appropriate commands. **(2 marks)**

4 Accept any two appropriate exclamations. These must start with 'How' or 'What' and contain a verb.

  (2 marks)

5 Answers will vary. Examples:
  a. <u>Eat/Finish</u> your breakfast immediately! **(1 mark)**
  b. <u>Stop/Stand</u> at the pedestrian crossing and <u>look</u> both ways before you cross. **(1 mark)**
  c. <u>Finish/Do</u> your homework then <u>give</u> it to your teacher. **(1 mark)**
  d. <u>Write/Send</u> a thank-you note to your friends who bought you presents. **(1 mark)**

6 (4 marks)

Sentence	Statement	Question	Command	Exclamation
Take the first road on the left, then turn left.			✓	
How many more days until the holidays?		✓		
What massive teeth that crocodile has!				✓
It's a perfect day for a picnic.	✓			

7 Answers will vary. Examples:
   a. How many children are there in your
     school? **(1 mark)**
   b. Where did you go on holiday last
     summer? **(1 mark)**
   c. Which way is the train station? **(1 mark)**

SENTENCE FEATURES

Subject–Verb agreement
pages 28–29

1 **a.** <u>Finn</u> watched the netball match. **(1 mark)**
   b. Last week, <u>my friends and I</u> took the
     bus home. **(1 mark)**
   c. After a while, <u>Sasha</u> stopped talking
     and listened to the teacher. **(1 mark)**
   d. <u>The rain</u> lashed continuously all through
     the night. **(1 mark)**
   e. Whenever <u>we</u> can, <u>my sisters and I</u> help
     our mum with the washing-up. **(1 mark)**
   f. <u>You</u> have eaten all the chocolates!
     (1 mark)

2 **b.** Aisha and Will doesn't have packed
     lunches with them today. ✓
     <u>Aisha and Will do not have packed</u>
     <u>lunches with them today.</u> **(1 mark)**

3 **a.** I was hungry. **(1 mark)**
   b. She was ten years old. **(1 mark)**
   c. They were sad. **(1 mark)**
   d. They went to bed early. **(1 mark)**
   e. She went to school on the bus. **(1 mark)**
   f. I went swimming every day. **(1 mark)**

4 **a.** We walked towards the cliff edge and
     took care that the wind didn't blow our
     hats off. **(1 mark)**
   b. As you discovered, the water was very
     deep in the harbour. **(1 mark)**
   c. She took great care when she drew
     diagrams. **(1 mark)**
   d. At 6 o'clock in the morning, is it any
     wonder I am too tired to eat? **(1 mark)**
   e. Sol runs over the finish line then throws
     himself on the ground in relief. **(1 mark)**
   f. We often watch animated films on TV but
     they are much better at the cinema.
     (1 mark)

Subject and object
pages 30–31

1 **a.** <u>My parents</u> love watching (the football)
     (1 mark)
   b. <u>A wasp</u> has just stung (me). **(1 mark)**
   c. <u>The three children</u> pushed
     (the garden gate). **(1 mark)**
   d. <u>The policeman</u> arrested (the thief).
     (1 mark)
   e. <u>The horses</u> were eating (hay). **(1 mark)**
   f. <u>My meddling little brother</u> has
     broken (my computer). **(1 mark)**

2 Accept six appropriate sentences containing
   both a subject and an object. **(6 marks)**

3 **a.** There are ten girls skipping. ✓ **(1 mark)**

4 Accept appropriate sentences. Examples:
   a. My mum likes baking **chocolate cakes**.
     (1 mark)
   b. Do you like drawing **cartoon pictures**?
     (1 mark)
   c. My sister is great at riding **horses**
     and ponies. **(1 mark)**
   d. We've all been playing **card and**
     board games. **(1 mark)**

Active and passive voice
pages 32–33

1 Accept two appropriate sentences in the
   active voice, e.g. The children went to
   school on the bus. **(2 marks)**

2 Accept two appropriate sentences in the
   passive voice, e.g. The boys were taken to
   the match by their dads. **(2 marks)**

3 **a.** The children were taken by their parents
     to the disco for the Year 6 treat.
     OR: The children were taken to the disco
     for the Year 6 treat. **(1 mark)**
   b. Everest was conquered by Sir Edmund
     Hillary and Sherpa Tenzing in 1953.
     OR: Everest was conquered in 1953 by
     Sir Edmund Hillary and Sherpa Tenzing.
     (1 mark)

c. The apple pie was burned by the cooks because the oven was too hot. **(1 mark)**

d. The rubbish was thrown out by Millie when the bin started to overflow. **(1 mark)**

e. My big sister's tooth was extracted by the dentist. **(1 mark)**

f. Finally, the Champion's Cup was won by the determined junior team.
OR: The Champion's Cup was finally won by the determined junior team. **(1 mark)**

4

Sentence	Active voice	Passive voice
The angry wasps stung the children.	✓	
My mother brought my friends and me to the cinema.	✓	
A family was rescued from the blaze by a fireman.		✓
We were given an ultimatum by our teacher.		✓
The thieves were being pursued.		✓
We left our picnic blanket by the edge of the river.	✓	

(6 marks)

5 a. An enthusiastic dog-walker walked my energetic dog all week.
OR: All week, an enthusiastic dog-walker walked my energetic dog. **(1 mark)**

b. The team completed the transatlantic race in record time. **(1 mark)**

c. The emergency team received three phone calls last night.
OR: Last night, the emergency team received three phone calls. **(1 mark)**

d. The young journalist wrote a fascinating newspaper article. **(1 mark)**

Direct speech
pages 34–35

1 When Benji heard the thunder in the middle of the night, he said it was the loudest noise he'd ever heard. <u>"Make it go away!"</u> he shouted. His mum said that it couldn't hurt him and it might help to count the seconds between the thunder claps and the lightning bolts. <u>"It's nature, sweetheart, and it won't last forever,"</u> she reassured him. <u>"Come on, let's count together."</u> <u>"One, two, three, four…"</u> they counted. By eight, Benji was already asleep. **(3 marks)**

2 a. "I would really like to go to the cinema to see that new Spiderman film," Paul said. **(1 mark)**

b. "We knew that eventually we would move to America," the children told their neighbours. **(1 mark)**

c. "Start running now!" Jack screamed. **(1 mark)**

d. Taylor said, "I hope I remembered to put the chocolate brownies in the picnic basket." **(1 mark)**

e. "Have you brought your library book in today?" asked the librarian. **(1 mark)**

3 a. "Will you play football with me, Billy?" asked Max. **(1 mark)**

b. "Everyone can come to my house for tea!" announced Harry. **(1 mark)**

c. "Score!" shouted all the Year 6 spectators to the lacrosse team. **(1 mark)**

d. "Could I have some extra time in the reading test?" Honor asked her teacher. **(1 mark)**

4 Answers will vary. Examples:
whispered; muttered; sighed; agreed; stuttered; uttered; shouted; roared; screamed; shrieked
(up to 10 marks)

Informal and formal speech
pages 36–37

1 a. Informal speech is a relaxed way of speaking where we might use slang, abbreviations and colloquialisms. In formal speech we use Standard English, applying all the rules of English grammar. **(2 marks)**

b. We use informal speech or writing when chatting, texting or emailing friends and family.
We use formal speech or writing when talking or writing to our teachers, other adults beyond our family or when delivering a speech. **(2 marks)**

2 a. informal **(1 mark)**
b. formal **(1 mark)**
c. informal **(1 mark)**
d. formal **(1 mark)**
e. informal **(1 mark)**
f. informal **(1 mark)**
g. formal **(1 mark)**

3 Answers will vary. Appropriate use of informal language, slang and colloquialisms. Examples:

Saturday
Got up dead late, stuffed my breakfast down me and hopped on the 214 bus to town. Met Bryony for a cuppa – hot choc, my fave!

Sunday
Watched the team play footie. They won! YEAH! Got home, grabbed a butty then met Bryony again 'coz she needed help with the well hard homework that the dragon set this week.

(4 marks)

4 a. Her Majesty requires that all visitors **be** respectful of the palace grounds. **(1 mark)**

b. If only we **were** able to join you on holiday! **(1 mark)**

5 Answers will vary. Example:
Good morning everybody. I'd like to extend a warm welcome to author Joseph Welsh. As many of you know from reading his books, Joseph writes adventure stories, often based on his own experiences. As a young child, Joseph… etc. **(4 marks)**

6 a. We aren't going to the park because we have visitors. **(1 mark)**

b. Pick those books up now or else I'll be very cross. **(1 mark)**

c. She would have helped you if you had asked. **(1 mark)**

d. I don't want any chips with my chicken. **(1 mark)**

PUNCTUATION

Capital letters and full stops
pages 38–39

1 We use punctuation marks as 'signposts' to help us understand a text. **(1 mark)**

2 We use capital letters at the start of a sentence and for proper nouns; full stops come at the end of a sentence. **(1 mark)**

3 **W**hen **M**aggie and **J**ack reached the outskirts of **L**ondon, they were quite overwhelmed at the sight of some of the iconic buildings. **L**ooming before them were the **H**ouses of **P**arliament, then **B**ig **B**en, next **W**estminster **A**bbey and **S**t. **P**aul's **C**athedral. **T**aking a boat on the **R**iver **T**hames, the children were wide-eyed in awe and amazement as they saw the city from a different perspective. **A**ll they could think about was how impressed their teacher, **M**rs **M**uggins, would be when they went in to school on **M**onday morning. **(4 marks)**

4

Sentence	Correct?
My brother said his friend pat was going to watch the new harry potter film with him.	
At breezybank primary school, the best teachers, in my opinion, are mrs mason and mr burns.	
after a long wait in London, the children got on the bus to Cambridge and went home.	
My next adventure will be to take a raft down the River Ganges in India.	✓
Every wednesday, I go to the swimming baths with Claire and Sam.	

(1 mark)

5 a. "I'm off to the shops now," said Bill to his sister. "There's a special discount on at Sweetsavers." **(1 mark)**

b. We couldn't understand how Maddie had forgotten her homework for the second time in a week. Our teacher had told her many times. **(1 mark)**

c. Looking out of the window, Tom was struggling to see his dad's Volvo through the fog. Then it started to clear and before he knew it Tom was outside playing in the sunshine. **(1 mark)**

d. Megan and Amy were off to Paris to visit the Eiffel Tower, which they hoped to climb to the top. They were going with their cousin Arthur who speaks French fluently. **(1 mark)**

e. I watched The Lion King when we went to London. It was truly amazing and probably the best performance I've ever seen. I would actually go back and watch it again. **(1 mark)**

Question marks and exclamation marks
pages 40–41

1 We use question marks to show someone has asked a question. **(1 mark)**

2 We use exclamation marks to show someone is exclaiming or sometimes when giving a command. **(1 mark)**

3 **a.** What dreadful weather it was! **(1 mark)**

 b. "I'm going home now, aren't you?" **(1 mark)**

 c. "There's not much point in staying any longer, is there?" **(1 mark)**

 d. How shocked we were to hear about the floods! **(1 mark)**

 e. Had they really arrived that morning in glorious sunshine? **(1 mark)**

4 Accept any suitable answers. Examples:

 a. What did the man look like? **(1 mark)**

 b. Who did you see in the park? **(1 mark)**

 c. How did you make that meal? **(1 mark)**

 d. When do you like to read? **(1 mark)**

5 **b.** Isn't it amazing to think that soon we will see another astronaut land on the Moon? ✓

 e. The pain in my leg is so excruciatingly bad I can hardly breathe. ✓

 (2 marks)

6 **a.** The weather's gone really cold, <u>hasn't it?</u> **(1 mark)**

 b. We are surely going to beat this team, <u>aren't we?</u> **(1 mark)**

 c. Last time we rode our scooters to the park, you fell off, <u>didn't you?</u> **(1 mark)**

 d. I don't think I've ever told you how grateful I am for your help, <u>have I?</u> **(1 mark)**

Commas
pages 42–43

1 Answers will vary. Examples:

 To separate items in a list; to indicate a brief pause in a sentence to make the meaning clearer and avoid ambiguity; before or after direct speech; to separate a clause from the rest of the sentence; to separate a fronted adverbial from the rest of the sentence.

 (4 marks)

2 **a.** Alfie consulted the recipe book and noted he would need sultanas, sugar, eggs, plain flour and cherries. **(1 mark)**

 b. The animals at the zoo ranged from fierce-looking tigers, hissing snakes and cheeky chimps to elegant giraffes, squawking cockatoos and lazy lions. **(1 mark)**

 c. With only minutes to spare before the flight, we threw our thermal vests, ski socks, fur-lined gloves and scarves into our cases, bags and rucksacks. **(1 mark)**

3 **a.** "Let's eat, Erin!" exclaimed a very hungry Milo. **(1 mark)**

 b. My friend's hobbies are cooking, her family and her pets. **(1 mark)**

 c. The pupil, thinks the teacher, is improving in Maths. **(1 mark)**

 d. The boy walked on, his head throbbing in pain. **(1 mark)**

 e. "That's a foul, striker!" shouted the referee. **(1 mark)**

4 **a.** "We really do need to get our skates on," said Mum. **(1 mark)**

 b. I looked at her in surprise and replied, "But surely we have two hours before it starts?" **(1 mark)**

 c. Mum raised her eyebrows, saying, "The traffic will be horrendous at this time of night." **(1 mark)**

 d. "Well, why don't we get the train? We could relax then and read our books," I suggested. **(1 mark)**

 e. "There's one at 7:08 from our local station," Mum said. **(1 mark)**

5 Answers will vary. Examples:

 a. We all trooped outside, **although it was raining heavily,** and played until our parents shouted at us to come inside. **(1 mark)**

 b. My collection of stamps, **which I kept in a leather-bound album,** sold on the Internet for an amazing sum of money. **(1 mark)**

 c. The neighbours to our right, **whose garden has always been a mess,** finally mowed their lawn and weeded their flower beds. **(1 mark)**

 d. My uncle Ted, **who is in his eighties,** still managed to run the London Marathon. **(1 mark)**

Inverted commas
pages 44–45

1 **a.** In direct speech, to indicate the start and end of someone speaking. **(1 mark)**

 b. For quotations. **(1 mark)**

 c. For nicknames and other titles. **(1 mark)**

2 **a.** "I've just discovered that our cousins are coming for the weekend," said Brogan. **(1 mark)**

 b. Joe was delighted and said, "We should take them to the forest and go exploring!" **(1 mark)**

 c. "Yes, let's build a den too!" exclaimed Brogan excitedly. "We'll have to take a picnic." **(1 mark)**

 d. "I'm not sure Sarah will come," said Joe. "Not after last time." **(1 mark)**

 e. "The incident with the spider wasn't my fault," responded Brogan defensively. **(1 mark)**

3 **b.** "I've just eaten two cakes and a packet of crisps", Rita told Dev. ✓

 d. "We have to go now"! Dad said firmly, "Otherwise we will be late." ✓

 (2 marks)

Answers

4
a. The boy they call "Mad Max" has just been seen hurtling towards the park.
Reason: <u>Nickname</u> **(2 marks)**

b. I've just finished reading "Harry Potter and the Philosopher's Stone".
Reason: <u>Book title</u> **(2 marks)**

c. Last night we watched "The Simpsons" on television.
Reason: <u>Title of programme</u> **(2 marks)**

d. The song I loved best at the concert was "One Way or Another".
Reason: <u>Song title</u> **(2 marks)**

e. I've just read an article about the Queen. One quote says: "Her Majesty is always in bed by ten." Another says: "Her Majesty likes cereal and toast for breakfast."
Reason: <u>Quotations</u> **(2 marks)**

Apostrophes
pages 46–47

1 She's always late for school. **(1 mark)**

2 My mum's birthday is today. **(1 mark)**

3

Word in full	Contraction	Word in full	Contraction
We have	**We've**	They are	**They're**
There is	**There's**	I would	**I'd**
She is	**She's**	I am	**I'm**
will not	**won't**	was not	**wasn't**
would have	**would've**	should not	**shouldn't**
is not	**isn't**	shall not	**shan't**

(6 marks)

4 b. We'll probably go to the caravan where there's always so much to do. ✓ **(1 mark)**

5 a. Mrs Smith's umbrella. **(1 mark)**
b. Sinead's homework was ruined by the rain. **(1 mark)**
c. The sun's rays beat down on the arid desert sand. **(1 mark)**
d. That dog's barks could be heard for miles and miles. **(1 mark)**
e. The girls' books need to go back to the library today. **(1 mark)**
f. Our class's furniture is going to be replaced. **(1 mark)**

6 a. It's almost dark so its best we head home before it's too late to catch the bus. **(3 marks)**
✓ ✗ ✓

b. Its been drizzling on and off all day so it's time the weather made it's mind up. **(3 marks)**
✗ ✓ ✗

Punctuation to indicate parenthesis
pages 48–49

1 a. The children's books (all of which are a bit tatty and worn) have finally been returned to the school library. **(1 mark)**
b. My brother Miles (the one who's mad about music) is going to a concert tonight. **(1 mark)**
c. How could anyone (even the most hard-hearted) not look at that newborn puppy and smile? **(1 mark)**
d. I've said before (and no doubt I will say it many times again) that I don't like being teased by my big sister. **(1 mark)**
e. Look in the far corner of the park (the spot where there's a fountain) and you will see the lads playing football. **(1 mark)**
f. I'm very good at reading (and writing for that matter) but I don't perform well in tests. **(1 mark)**

2 Answers will vary. Examples:
b. With only minutes to spare – **two to be exact** – we managed to get the last train. **(1 mark)**
c. Imagine my delight when chicken and carrots – **my favourite** – were served on the plane. **(1 mark)**
d. The winning goal – **scored by Rooney** – was the best of the match. **(1 mark)**
e. My best friend's dad – **Mr Weasley** – took us to school this morning. **(1 mark)**
f. We went to the local cinema – **the Odeon** – to watch the new Disney film. **(1 mark)**

3 d. My brother, short but very strong, stopped the thieves from getting away. ✓ **(1 mark)**

10 Answers

Colons, semi-colons, dashes and bullet points

pages 50–51

1 **a.** You will need the following: scissors, glue, paper, paint and water. **(1 mark)**

   b. I have only one dream: to play for a Premier League team. **(1 mark)**

   c. The Head Teacher made her last announcement of the evening: there would be tea and coffee served in the staffroom. **(1 mark)**

   d. Narrator: Tonight, thankfully, was not to be Bird Pie Night! **(1 mark)**

2 **a.** I've always loved the idea of living by the sea; in time, I'm sure, we'll make the move. **(1 mark)**

   b. There were children from all over the world on the residential trip: Helga from Frankfurt in Germany; Berndt from Zurich in Switzerland; Manuel from Lisbon in Portugal and Rory from Belfast in Northern Ireland. **(2 marks)**

3 **a.** Finally, we were at the top of the highest mountain in the world – now for the descent. **(1 mark)**

   b. I had reached the end of my magical journey – or was it *really* the end? **(1 mark)**

   c. The Maths paper was very hard – so hard that I think I've failed. **(1 mark)**

   d. I turned a corner and surveyed the scene – a horror that words could not describe. **(1 mark)**

4 Answers will vary. Examples:

   a. To make beans on toast you will need the following ingredients:
   - beans
   - bread
   - butter **(1 mark)**

   b. Before going on holiday, the children packed the following:
   - towels
   - swimwear
   - shorts **(1 mark)**

   c. My top four favourite celebrities are the following:
   - Harry Styles
   - Taylor Swift
   - Daniel Radcliffe
   - David Beckham **(1 mark)**

Hyphens and ellipses

pages 52–53

1

A	B	C
kind	minded	kind-hearted
well	tempered	well-known
fair	living	fair-minded
dark	coloured	dark-haired
long	known	long-living
multi	hearted	multi-coloured
bad	haired	bad-tempered

(7 marks)

2 **a.** re-form **(1 mark)**

   b. re-present **(1 mark)**

   c. re-cover **(1 mark)**

3 **a.** Rebecca stared out of the window and considered her options... she could stay or she could go. **(1 mark)**

   b. As Joe approached the cave, he heard a groaning noise… or maybe it was a growl. **(1 mark)**

   c. Standing on the top diving board, Jake held his breath and looked down at the pool... then he jumped. **(1 mark)**

4 Ellipsis is used to show that there is text between the last word before the ellipsis and the first word after the ellipsis. **(1 mark)**

VOCABULARY AND SPELLING

Synonyms and antonyms

pages 54–55

Synonyms

1 A synonym is a word with the same or a similar meaning as another word. **(1 mark)**

2 Answers may vary. Examples:

Adjectives	Synonyms	Nouns	Synonyms
noisy	**loud**	present	**gift**
angry	**cross**	bravery	**courage**
delicious	**tasty**	drink	**beverage**
scary	**frightening**	argument	**quarrel**
untidy	**messy**	drawing	**sketch**
easy	**straightforward**	walk	**stroll**

(12 marks)

3 Answers may vary. Examples:

   a. exclaimed **(1 mark)**

   b. strolled **(1 mark)**

   c. sketched **(1 mark)**

   d. baked **(1 mark)**

   e. disrupted **(1 mark)**

   f. irritates **(1 mark)**

Antonyms

1 An antonym is a word opposite in meaning
to another word. **(1 mark)**

2 **c.** My dog's bed consists of a large cushion
and **firm** sides. ☑ **(1 mark)**

3 Answers may vary. Examples:
   a. cold; heavy **(1 mark)**
   b. bright; powerful **(1 mark)**
   c. raised; over **(1 mark)**

Prefixes
pages 56–57

1 A prefix is a string of letters added to the
start of a word to turn it into another word.
(1 mark)

2

Prefix	Word	New word
il	accessible	**illogical**
ir	ability	**irrespective**
dis	apprehension	**disability**
mis	logical	**misapprehension**
im	respective	**implausible**
in	plausible	**inaccessible**

(6 marks)

3 **a.** disrespect **(1 mark)**
   b. misrepresent **(1 mark)**
   c. disagree **(1 mark)**
   d. misunderstanding **(1 mark)**
   e. misinterpreted **(1 mark)**

4 Not functioning correctly. **(1 mark)**

5 **b.** The teacher said my artwork was
   incomplete. ☑ **(1 mark)**
   d. It is quite improbable that the stadium will
   be finished by next year. ☑ **(1 mark)**

Prefixes from Latin and Greek

1 **a.** two **(1 mark)**
   b. big / above **(1 mark)**
   c. distant / far **(1 mark)**
   d. half **(1 mark)**

2 Answers may vary. Examples:

auto		aqua	pre
autobiography	autograph	aquaplane	preview
autocratic/ autocracy	automatic	aquamarine	premeditated
automobile	autopilot	aquarium	predate

(12 marks)

Suffixes
pages 58–59

1 A suffix is a letter string added to the end
of a root word, changing or adding to its
meaning. **(1 mark)**

2

	Adjective	Adverb
depend	**dependable**	**dependably**
comfort	**comfortable**	**comfortably**
rely	**reliable**	**reliably**
notice	**noticeable**	**noticeably**

(4 marks)

3

	Adjective	Adverb
horror	**horrible**	**horribly**
terror	**terrible**	**terribly**
sense	**sensible**	**sensibly**
reverse	**reversible**	**reversibly**
audio	**audible**	**audibly**

(5 marks)

4 **a.** vicious **(1 mark)**
   b. malicious **(1 mark)**
   c. spacious **(1 mark)**
   d. gracious **(1 mark)**

5 **a.** ambitious **(1 mark)**
   b. infectious **(1 mark)**
   c. nutritious **(1 mark)**
   d. fictitious **(1 mark)**

Suffixes
pages 60–61

1 **a.** residential **(1 mark)**
   b. financial **(1 mark)**
   c. influential **(1 mark)**
   d. facial **(1 mark)**

2 **a.** innocence **(1 mark)**
   b. defence **(1 mark)**
   c. dominance **(1 mark)**
   d. tolerance **(1 mark)**
   e. hesitance **(1 mark)**
   f. obedience **(1 mark)**

3 **a.** Walking in the Peak District was a real
   endurance test. **(1 mark)**
   b. The Head Teacher thanked us for our
   compliance with the school uniform rule.
   (1 mark)
   c. My **reliance** on my brother to help me
   with my homework has got to stop!
   (1 mark)

d. The instructions said that after the **appliance** of glue, the two sides would stick together.   **(1 mark)**

e. After much **reassurance** from my friends, I felt able to confront the bully.   **(1 mark)**

f. The **disappearance** of our dog in the middle of the night was a complete mystery.   **(1 mark)**

4 a. interference   **(1 mark)**
b. perseverance   **(1 mark)**
c. adherence   **(1 mark)**

Suffixes from Greek

1 Answers will vary. Examples:

Suffix	Word	Meaning
phone	xylophone	A percussion instrument
meter	pedometer	A device which measures how far you run, walk or cycle
logy	geology	The study of rocks
phobia	agoraphobia	A fear of public places

(8 marks)

Tricky spellings

pages 62–63

The rule 'i before e except after c but only when it rhymes with bee'

1 Answers will vary. Examples:
field; piece; shield; ceiling; deceive; conceive

(6 marks)

2 a. receipt   **(1 mark)**
b. deceive   **(1 mark)**
c. perceived   **(1 mark)**
d. ceiling   **(1 mark)**
e. conceived   **(1 mark)**
f. received   **(1 mark)**

3 a. eight   **(1 mark)**
b. weight   **(1 mark)**
c. beige   **(1 mark)**
d. weird   **(1 mark)**
e. protein   **(1 mark)**
f. caffeine   **(1 mark)**

Words ending in fer

1

Word	Add suffixes	Is the **fer** stressed?
refer	referral	✓
	reference	✗
	referred	✓
transfer	transferral	✓
	transference	✗
	transferred	✓
prefer	preference	✗
	preferred	✓
infer	inference	✗
	inferred	✓

(10 marks)

Tricky spellings

pages 64–65

Letter string ough

1 Answers will vary. Examples:

oh sound	aw sound	uff sound	ow sound	o sound
although	brought	rough	plough	trough
dough	thought	tough	drought	

(1 mark per word)

2 a. My brother **brought** me some **cough** medicine because he **thought** it would make me better.   **(1 mark)**

b. The **rough** seas were bad **enough** but once on land, a **bough** from a **tough** old oak tree snapped and landed on my head.   **(1 mark)**

Silent letters

1 A silent letter is a letter that we don't pronounce.   **(1 mark)**

2 a. assi<u>g</u>n   **b.** de<u>b</u>t   **c.** crum<u>b</u>
d. nes<u>t</u>le   **e.** condem<u>n</u>   **f.** <u>h</u>onest
g. forei<u>g</u>n   **h.** s<u>w</u>ord   **i.** <u>k</u>nowledge
j. hym<u>n</u>   **k.** s<u>c</u>issors   **l.** recei<u>p</u>t

(12 marks)

3 a. Wednesday   handkerchief   **(1 mark)**
b. jostling   silhouette   **(1 mark)**
c. receipt   succumbing   **(1 mark)**
d. solemn   echoed   **(1 mark)**

The prefix psych

1 a. psychology   **(1 mark)**
b. psychiatrist   **(1 mark)**
c. psychic   **(1 mark)**
d. psychedelic   **(1 mark)**

The letters ph

1 Answers will vary. Examples:
pharaoh, pharmacy, photo, phrase, physical, physics
alphabet, apostrophe, graph, geography, sphere, trophy   **(12 marks)**

Tricky plurals
pages 66–67
Words ending in o
1

Singular	Plural
piano	**pianos**
hero	**heroes**
mango	**mangos / mangoes**
studio	**studios**
banjo	**banjos / banjoes**
echo	**echoes**
kilo	**kilos**
potato	**potatoes**
torpedo	**torpedoes**

(9 marks)

Words ending in f, ff and fe

1 a. shelves   **(1 mark)**
   b. knives   **(1 mark)**
   c. lives   **(1 mark)**
   d. wolves   **(1 mark)**
   e. thieves   **(1 mark)**

2 a. The tribal <u>chiefs</u> agreed to respect each others' different <u>beliefs</u>.   **(1 mark)**
   b. From the top of the <u>roofs</u> came billowing <u>puffs</u> of white smoke.   **(1 mark)**
   c. The pirate's <u>bluffs</u> had gone on long enough so the captain dropped anchor in front of the towering white <u>cliffs</u> and confronted him.   **(1 mark)**
   d. The garden party <u>chefs</u> put on <u>waterproofs</u> when it started to rain.   **(1 mark)**
   e. The little <u>waifs</u> were poorly dressed and underfed after being looked after by two beastly <u>oafs</u>.   **(1 mark)**

Words with two possible plurals
1

Singular	Plural 1	Plural 2
scarf	**scarves**	**scarfs**
wharf	**wharves**	**wharfs**
dwarf	**dwarves**	**dwarfs**
hoof	**hooves**	**hoofs**

(4 marks)

Homophones
pages 68–69
Homophones

1 A homophone is a word that sounds the same as another word but has a different spelling and different meaning.   **(1 mark)**

2 d. I looked **through** the window and saw a huge **bear** ambling about in the garden. ☑   **(1 mark)**

3

Word	Homophone(s)	Word	Homophone(s)
pause	**paws**	whether	**weather**
piece	**peace**	find	**fined**
pour	**pore / poor**	great	**grate**
knew	**new / gnu**	shore	**sure**
buy	**bye / by**	night	**knight**
morning	**mourning**	sent	**scent / cent**
profit	**prophet**	root	**route**

(14 marks)

4 a. We walked down the **main** road to get to the bus stop.   **(1 mark)**
   b. **There** was a lot of traffic as it was rush hour.   **(1 mark)**
   c. In addition, there was a hold up **due** to roadworks.   **(1 mark)**
   d. We **guessed** that our bus would be very late.   **(1 mark)**
   d. So we **proceeded** to walk to school instead.   **(1 mark)**

Near homophones

1 Near homophones don't sound exactly the same but are similar enough for people often to misspell them.   **(1 mark)**

2 a. The hot, sunny weather had a therapeutic (effect) on the whole family.   **(1 mark)**
   b. The teacher gave the parents some great (advice) about the tests.   **(1 mark)**
   c. The fireman couldn't gain (access) to the burning building.   **(1 mark)**
   d. Last night the swimming pool was full of screaming (adolescents)   **(1 mark)**
   e. I bought the latest (edition) of my favourite magazine.   **(1 mark)**
   f. We all found it difficult to (accept) that our cat had gone.   **(1 mark)**

pages 70–78

1 Any suitable answer, such as:
   <u>because</u> / <u>since</u> / <u>as</u> / <u>while</u> **(1 mark)**

2 fell ☑ **(1 mark)**

3 irresponsible ☑ **(1 mark)**

4 The thieves were arrested as they tried to leave town. ☑ **(1 mark)**

5 <u>Cautiously</u>, the boys crept into the cave, treading carefully as they went. **(1 mark)**

6 <u>When Sonia arrived at her dad's bedside,</u> she could see that he had improved. **(1 mark)**

   she → adjective ... he → noun

7 Phil studied the detailed map then put it back neatly in his waterproof rucksack. **(1 mark)**

   detailed → adjective ... map → noun

8 an exclamation ☑ **(1 mark)**

9 **a.** Answers will vary. Example:
      A word that means the same / nearly the same as another word. **(1 mark)**

   b. Any suitable answer, such as:
      exhausted, wrecked **(1 mark)**

10 Our football team finally won (but) we know we have a long way to go (before) we can claim the league cup. **(1 mark)**

11

Sentence	Present progressive	Past progressive
My sisters were eating jam and toast.		✓
Ushma's dog was teasing my cat.		✓
The boys are swimming in the sea early this morning.	✓	

(1 mark)

12 I have; weather is; we have **(1 mark)**

13 My younger brother loves peas (yet) hates carrots. **(1 mark)**

14 **a.** dashes / double dashes **(1 mark)**
   b. (a pair of) commas or (a pair of) brackets **(1 mark)**

15 We met a lovely family on holiday last year**;** we are meeting up with them again this year. **(1 mark)**

16 My dog jumped (over) the gate and ran (into) the field. **(1 mark)**

17 My brother went to school today, <u>although he has his arm in plaster</u>. **(1 mark)**

18 "So you think you're going to win the match tomorrow, <u>do you</u>?" **(1 mark)**

19 "Hurry up or you'll be late for school!" shouted my mum. "It's almost 9 o'clock." **(1 mark)**

20 **a.** Mum has been waiting for ages for Katie's bus but (it's) clearly late. **(1 mark)**
   b. We're thrilled that (Jake's) birthday celebration wasn't ruined by the bad weather. **(1 mark)**

21

Sentence	Main clause	Subordinate clause
Claudie went home early <u>because she was tired</u>.		✓
<u>Mrs Smith</u>, who used to be my teacher, <u>visited us in school today</u>.	✓	
<u>We will go to the beach</u> if the weather improves.	✓	

(1 mark)

22 Stella's reading is more advanced than Chloe's. ☑ **(1 mark)**

23 When I go away for a weekend in the countryside, I always pack the following: sweaters, boots, gloves and a coat. **(1 mark)**

24 Now that we **have eaten** our breakfast, we can set off on our journey. **(1 mark)**

25 were ☑ **(1 mark)**

26 I will finish my homework project this evening. ☑ **(1 mark)**

27 You need to water the flowers **and** the plants, **even though** it rained in the night. Here is a watering can **but** you might prefer to use a jug **or** a hose. **(1 mark)**

28 (Our house) has a south-facing garden. **(1 mark)**

29 Shall we start to eat, Mum?
   The speaker is asking their mum if they should start to eat.
   Shall we start to eat Mum?
   The speaker is asking someone else if they should start to eat their mum. **(1 mark)**

30 After an extremely long flight, I was relieved to get into my comfortable bed for a sleep. **(1 mark)**

31 write or draw ☑ **(1 mark)**

32 There isn't time for us to eat because **it's** already 9 o'clock. **(1 mark)**

33 Mrs Courtney's antique vase suddenly tipped over. **(1 mark)**

   C D A B

34 Are the children going to bed? **(1 mark)**

35

Sentence	Apostrophe used in a contraction	Apostrophe used to show possession
I daren't tell the teacher I forgot my homework.	✓	
Rebecca's pony likes apples.		✓
The children's books are in the library.		✓

(1 mark)

36 illegal **(1 mark)**

37 As we **were walking** along the beach, we saw some birds which **were flying** high in the sky. **(1 mark)**

38 accident ✓ **(1 mark)**

39 <u>Turn</u> to the next page and <u>read</u> the first two paragraphs. What do you think made Theo react that way? **(1 mark)**

40 Mrs Rothwell's computer screen needed to be fixed. **(1 mark)**

5 Tick **two** boxes to indicate the sentences which are correctly punctuated. **(2 marks)**

a. I really thought you, of all people, would have behaved more sensibly? ☐

b. Isn't it amazing to think that soon we will see another astronaut land on the Moon? ☐

c. Go away – you deliberately pushed me over when I was trying to score? ☐

d. I'm so excited about our trip to New York next week, aren't you! ☐

e. The pain in my leg is so excruciatingly bad I can hardly breathe. ☐

6 Add suitable **question tags** to the following sentences, finishing with the correct **punctuation**.

An example has been done for you.

You have tidied your bedroom, *haven't you?*...............

a. The weather's gone really cold, ... **(1 mark)**

b. We are surely going to beat this team, ... **(1 mark)**

c. Last time we rode our scooters to the park, you fell off, ... **(1 mark)**

d. I don't think I've ever told you how grateful I am for your help, ... **(1 mark)**

You might see small **i** for **I** used in a text message but you should only ever write it with a capital **I**!

Top tip!

1 Write four places where you might use **commas**.

a. .... **(1 mark)**

b. .... **(1 mark)**

c. .... **(1 mark)**

d. .... **(1 mark)**

2 Insert the missing **commas** in these sentences.

a. Alfie consulted the recipe book and noted he would need sultanas sugar eggs plain flour and cherries. **(1 mark)**

b. The animals at the zoo ranged from fierce-looking tigers hissing snakes and cheeky chimps to elegant giraffes squawking cockatoos and lazy lions. **(1 mark)**

c. With only minutes to spare before the flight, we threw our thermal vests ski socks fur-lined gloves and scarves into our cases bags and rucksacks. **(1 mark)**

3 Position **commas** in the following sentences to avoid ambiguity.

a. "Let's eat Erin!" exclaimed a very hungry Milo. **(1 mark)**

b. My friend's hobbies are cooking her family and her pets. **(1 mark)**

c. The pupil thinks the teacher is improving in Maths. **(1 mark)**

d. The boy walked on his head throbbing in pain. **(1 mark)**

e. "That's a foul striker!" shouted the referee. **(1 mark)**

4 Insert **commas** in the correct places in the following direct speech.

a. "We really do need to get our skates on " said Mum. **(1 mark)**

b. I looked at her in surprise and replied "But surely we have two hours before it starts?" **(1 mark)**

c. Mum raised her eyebrows, saying "The traffic will be horrendous at this time of night." **(1 mark)**

d. "Well, why don't we get the train? We could relax then and read our books " I suggested. **(1 mark)**

e. "There's one at 7:08 from our local station " Mum said. **(1 mark)**

5 Complete each sentence by writing a subordinate clause in the gap. Use the words in brackets. Add commas where you think they are needed. An example has been done for you.

The stooped, white-haired man, *who ran from the crime scene*., was asked to help the police with their investigation.

a. We all trooped outside (although) .... and played until our parents shouted at us to come inside. **(1 mark)**

b. My collection of stamps (which) .... sold on the Internet for an amazing sum of money. **(1 mark)**

c. The neighbours to our right (whose) .... finally mowed their lawn and weeded their flower beds. **(1 mark)**

d. My uncle Ted (who) .... still managed to run the London Marathon. **(1 mark)**

Commas are punctuation marks used to separate items in a list, clarify meaning, avoid ambiguity and indicate parenthesis; they can also be used in punctuating direct speech.

1 Write three places where we use **inverted commas**.

a. .... **(1 mark)**

b. .... **(1 mark)**

c. .... **(1 mark)**

2 Insert inverted commas and any other missing punctuation in the following direct speech.

a. I've just discovered that our cousins are coming for the weekend said Brogan. **(1 mark)**

b. Joe was delighted and said We should take them to the forest and go exploring! **(1 mark)**

c. Yes, let's build a den too exclaimed Brogan excitedly. We'll have to take a picnic. **(1 mark)**

d. I'm not sure Sarah will come said Joe Not after last time. **(1 mark)**

e. The incident with the spider wasn't my fault responded Brogan defensively. **(1 mark)**

3 Which **two** sentences are **not** correctly punctuated?
Tick **two**. **(2 marks)**

a. "How many environmental issues are on today's agenda?" asked the Year 6 House Captain. ☐

b. "I've just eaten two cakes and a packet of crisps", Rita told Dev. ☐

c. "I've not seen the cartoon you are talking about," Phil said. ☐

d. "We have to go now"! Dad said firmly, "Otherwise we will be late." ☐

e. "I've just seen our friends walking down the road with their new dog!" ☐

4 Inverted commas could be used in each of the following sentences. Rewrite them, inserting the inverted commas, and say why you have used them.

a. The boy they call Mad Max has just been seen hurtling towards the park. **(2 marks)**

....

Reason: ....

b. I've just finished reading Harry Potter and the Philosopher's Stone. **(2 marks)**

....

Reason: ....

c. Last night we watched The Simpsons on television. **(2 marks)**

....

Reason: ....

d. The song I loved best at the concert was One Way or Another. **(2 marks)**

....

Reason: ....

e. I've just read an article about the Queen. One quote says: Her Majesty is always in bed by ten. Another says: Her Majesty likes cereal and toast for breakfast. **(2 marks)**

....

....

Reason: ....

I'd like to watch "The Simpsons" tonight if I get my homework finished.

Top tip! Make sure your inverted commas sit at the right height on the line. They shouldn't look long and straggly like spiders' legs! The opening inverted commas should curve the opposite way to a comma and the closing inverted commas should look like two commas.

Total $\frac{}{20}$

1 Insert the missing **apostrophe** to show a **contraction** in the sentence below. **(1 mark)**

Shes always late for school.

2 Insert the missing **apostrophe** to show **possession** in the sentence below. **(1 mark)**

My mums birthday is today.

3 Use an **apostrophe** to turn the following words into **contractions**. **(6 marks)**

Word in full	Contraction	Word in full	Contraction
We have	....	They are	....
There is	....	I would	....
She is	....	I am	....
will not	....	was not	....
would have	....	should not	....
is not	....	shall not	....

4 Which sentence uses **apostrophes for contractions** correctly? **(1 mark)**

Tick the correct one.

a. Iv'e not had my holiday yet because my dads' been too busy at work. ☐

b. We'll probably go to the caravan where there's always so much to do. ☐

c. My cousins' coming to join us for two days which'll be fun. ☐

d. Ther'es not much else Iw'd rather do. ☐

5 Rewrite these sentences so that they contain **apostrophes to show possession**. The first one has been done for you.

The dog belonging to my best friend is really naughty.

My best friend's dog is really naughty.

a. The umbrella that belongs to Mrs Smith. **(1 mark)**

....

b. The homework belonging to Sinead was ruined by the rain. **(1 mark)**

....

c. The rays of the sun beat down on the arid desert sand. **(1 mark)**

....

d. The barks of that dog could be heard for miles and miles. **(1 mark)**

....

e. The books belonging to the girls need to go back to the library today. **(1 mark)**

....

f. The furniture belonging to our class is going to be replaced. **(1 mark)**

....

6 Decide whether the following have used **its** or **it's** correctly. Put a tick ✓ or cross ✗ in the boxes.

a. It's almost dark so its best we head home before it's too late to catch the bus.

⬜ ⬜ ⬜ **(3 marks)**

b. Its been drizzling on and off all day so it's time the weather made it's mind up.

⬜ ⬜ ⬜ **(3 marks)**

Remember that **it's** always means **it is** – it is never used to show possession! "The dog wagged **its** tail."

Top tip!

Total $\frac{}{21}$

1 Insert brackets to show **parenthesis** in each sentence.

a. The children's books all of which are a bit tatty and worn have finally been returned to the school library. **(1 mark)**

b. My brother Miles the one who's mad about music is going to a concert tonight. **(1 mark)**

c. How could anyone even the most hard-hearted not look at that newborn puppy and smile? **(1 mark)**

d. I've said before and no doubt I will say it many times again that I don't like being teased by my big sister. **(1 mark)**

e. Look in the far corner of the park the spot where there's a fountain and you will see the lads playing football. **(1 mark)**

f. I'm very good at reading and writing for that matter but I don't perform well in tests. **(1 mark)**

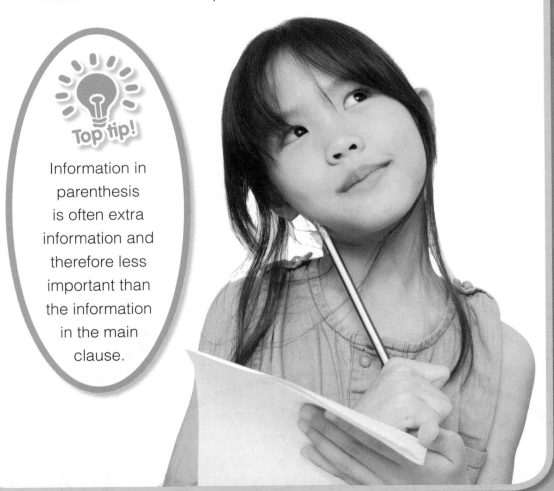

Top tip!

Information in parenthesis is often extra information and therefore less important than the information in the main clause.

2 Write a word, phrase or clause in each gap, using **dashes** around the parenthesis. The first one has been done for you.

a. After some time, we went home – *tired and muddy* – and had hot baths and bowls of soup.

b. With only minutes to spare .... we managed to get the last train. **(1 mark)**

c. Imagine my delight when chicken and carrots .... were served on the plane. **(1 mark)**

d. The winning goal .... was the best of the match. **(1 mark)**

e. My best friend's dad .... took us to school this morning. **(1 mark)**

f. We went to the local cinema .... to watch the new Disney film. **(1 mark)**

3 Which sentence uses commas correctly to show parenthesis? **(1 mark)**

Tick the correct sentence.

a. There was a lot, of fuss unnecessarily, after the ice-cream turned out to be the wrong flavour. ☐

b. Ruby not usually, a competitive girl, was first to fling herself over the finish line. ☐

c. When we reached the summit exhausted but exhilarated, we all cheered. ☐

d. My brother, short but very strong, stopped the thieves from getting away. ☐

> **Top tip!** The words in parenthesis are often relative clauses with the relative pronouns omitted. For example:
> My dinner, ready since 6 o'clock, was starting to turn cold.
> My dinner, which had been ready since 6 o'clock, was starting to turn cold.

Total ── 12

1 Insert **colons** in the correct places in the following.

a. You will need the following scissors, glue, paper, paint and water. **(1 mark)**

b. I have only one dream to play for a Premier League team. **(1 mark)**

c. The Head Teacher made her last announcement of the evening there would be tea and coffee served in the staffroom. **(1 mark)**

d. Narrator Tonight, thankfully, was not to be Bird Pie Night! **(1 mark)**

2 Insert **semi-colons** in the following sentences.

a. I've always loved the idea of living by the sea in time, I'm sure, we'll make the move. **(1 mark)**

b. There were children from all over the world on the residential trip: Helga from Frankfurt in Germany Berndt from Zurich in Switzerland Manuel from Lisbon in Portugal and Rory from Belfast in Northern Ireland. **(2 marks)**

3 Rewrite the following sentences so that they contain a **single dash**.

a. Finally, we were at the top of the highest mountain in the world now for the descent. **(1 mark)**

....

b. I had reached the end of my magical journey or was it *really* the end? **(1 mark)**

....

c. The Maths paper was very hard so hard that I think I've failed. **(1 mark)**

....

d. I turned a corner and surveyed the scene a horror that words could not describe. **(1 mark)**

....

4 Write suitable **bullet points** to follow on from these introductions.

a. To make beans on toast you will need the following ingredients: **(1 mark)**

....

....

....

b. Before going on holiday, the children packed the following: **(1 mark)**

....

....

....

c. My top four favourite celebrities are the following: **(1 mark)**

....

....

....

....

Top tip!

The text following the bullet points does not need to start with a capital letter or end with a full stop. However, if you **do** start with a capital letter, then end with a full stop!

Total $\frac{}{14}$

1 Match each word in column A to a word in column B to make compound words linked by a **hyphen**. Write these in column C. **(7 marks)**

A	B	C
kind	minded	....
well	tempered	....
fair	living	....
dark	coloured	....
long	known	....
multi	hearted	....
bad	haired	....

2 Change the meaning of these words by inserting a **hyphen** between the **prefix** and the root word.

An example has been done for you.

recollect   *re-collect*

a. reform   .... **(1 mark)**

b. represent   .... **(1 mark)**

c. recover .... **(1 mark)**

3 Rewrite the following pairs of sentences as one, inserting three dots to show ellipsis in each.

a. Rebecca stared out of the window and considered her options. She could stay or she could go. **(1 mark)**

....

....

b. As Joe approached the cave, he heard a groaning noise. Or maybe it was a growl. **(1 mark)**

....

....

c. Standing on the top diving board, Jake held his breath and looked down at the pool. Then he jumped. **(1 mark)**

....

....

4 Explain why **ellipsis** is used in this sentence. **(1 mark)**
Read the following passage on page 5: "Slowly then... arms."

....

....

....

Top tip!
Remember, only use three dots for ellipsis.

Total ─── 14

Synonyms

1 What is a **synonym**? **(1 mark)**

....

2 Find **synonyms** for the following adjectives and nouns. **(12 marks)**

Adjectives	Synonyms	Nouns	Synonyms
noisy	....	present	....
angry	....	bravery	....
delicious	....	drink	....
scary	....	argument	....
untidy	....	drawing	....
easy	....	walk	....

3 Choose a **synonym** to replace the verbs in bold.

a. "Let's go for a swim now!" **said** Marcus. **(1 mark)**

....

b. We **walked** to the village square to see the band. **(1 mark)**

....

c. The children **did** self-portraits in Art. **(1 mark)**

....

d. Mum **made** a cake this afternoon. **(1 mark)**

....

e. The naughty boy **disturbed** the whole class. **(1 mark)**

....

f. My sister **annoys** me every day. **(1 mark)**

....

Antonyms

1 What is an **antonym**? **(1 mark)**

....

2 Which sentence uses an antonym for the adjective **soft**? **(1 mark)**

Tick the correct sentence.

a. On Sunday mornings, I wrap myself in my fluffy, feathery duvet. ☐

b. The ball smashed through the window, leaving pointy shards of glass. ☐

c. My dog's bed consists of a large cushion and firm sides. ☐

d. The country road was long, muddy and bumpy. ☐

3 Write **antonyms** for the words in bold.

a. Yesterday was so **hot** that we wore **light** layers on our walk. **(1 mark)**

....

....

b. The lighting in here is very **dull** because the bulbs are so **weak**. **(1 mark)**

....

....

c. We **lowered** the injured dog until we could get him **under** the fence. **(1 mark)**

....

....

Total — 24

1 Explain what a **prefix** is. **(1 mark)**

....

2 Match each **prefix** with a word to make a new word that is opposite in meaning. **(6 marks)**

Prefix	Word	New word
il	accessible	....
ir	ability	....
dis	apprehension	....
mis	logical	....
im	respective	....
in	plausible	....

3 Rewrite the words in brackets to give them a negative meaning by adding the prefixes **dis** or **mis**.

a. He showed (respect) .... by calling out while the teacher was speaking. **(1 mark)**

b. We don't want to (represent) .... the facts by exaggerating. **(1 mark)**

c. Please don't (agree) .... with me because you know I'm right! **(1 mark)**

d. The whole thing has been a total (understanding) .... **(1 mark)**

e. I think you have (interpreted) .... what I was trying to say. **(1 mark)**

4 If you add the prefix **mal** to the word 'odorous', you make the word 'malodorous', meaning 'bad smelling'.

Add **mal** to the word 'practice' and you get 'malpractice', meaning 'bad practice'.

Now work out what **malfunction** means. **(1 mark)**

....

5 Tick the **two** sentences that use **prefixes** correctly.   **(2 marks)**

a. I think the football team were somewhat disguided by their coach.   ☐

b. The teacher said my artwork was incomplete.   ☐

c. Although the puppies are from the same litter, they are quite unsimilar.   ☐

d. It is quite improbable that the stadium will be finished by next year.   ☐

Prefixes from Latin and Greek

1 What do these **prefixes** mean?

a. bi   e.g. **bi**lingual; **bi**cycle   ....   **(1 mark)**

b. super   e.g. **super**market; **super**human   ....   **(1 mark)**

c. tele   e.g. **tele**scope; **tele**vision   ....   **(1 mark)**

d. semi   e.g. **semi**-circle; **semi**-detached   ....   **(1 mark)**

2 How many words can you think of that begin with the prefixes **auto**, **aqua** and **pre**?

(12 marks)

auto		aqua	pre
....	....	....	....
....	....	....	....
....	....	....	....

Top tip!

Anything with **anti** as its prefix is going to have an opposite meaning to the original word. 'Anti-clockwise' means the opposite to 'clockwise'.

Total $\frac{}{31}$

1 What is a **suffix**? **(1 mark)**

....

....

2 Add the suffixes **able** and **ably** to these words, to make adjectives and adverbs.

	Adjective	Adverb
depend	....	....
comfort	....	....
rely	....	....
notice	....	....

(4 marks)

3 Add the suffixes **ible** and **ibly** to these words to make adjectives and adverbs. **(5 marks)**

	Adjective	Adverb
horror	....	....
terror	....	....
sense	....	....
reverse	....	....
audio	....	....

4 Add the suffix **cious** to turn these nouns into adjectives.

a. vice .... **(1 mark)**

b. malice .... **(1 mark)**

c. space .... **(1 mark)**

d. grace .... **(1 mark)**

5 Add the suffix **tious** to turn these nouns into adjectives.

a. ambition .... **(1 mark)**

b. infection .... **(1 mark)**

c. nutrition .... **(1 mark)**

d. fiction .... **(1 mark)**

Total ——
18

❶ Rewrite the following sentences using either the suffix **tial** or **cial** to turn the nouns in bold into adjectives.

a. We went on our Year 6 (**residence**) trip to the Lake District.

(1 mark)

....

b. After so many (**finance**) worries, the Head Teacher was relieved he could afford the PE equipment. **(1 mark)**

....

c. Many people believed the teacher had been very (**influence**) in inspiring the children. **(1 mark)**

....

d. The cheeky boy pulled different (**face**) expressions as the teacher talked. **(1 mark)**

....

❷ Choose either the suffix **ence** or **ance** to change these words into nouns that you cannot see or touch.

a. innocent .... **(1 mark)**

b. defend .... **(1 mark)**

c. dominate .... **(1 mark)**

d. tolerate .... **(1 mark)**

e. hesitate .... **(1 mark)**

f. obedient .... **(1 mark)**

❸ Change these verbs into nouns by adding either the suffix **ence** or **ance**.

a. Walking in the Peak District was a real (**endure**) test.

.... **(1 mark)**

Top tip!

If a noun is formed from a verb ending in **y**, **ure** or **ear**, the ending of the noun will be **ance**. If a noun is formed from a verb ending in **ere** or **er**, the ending of the noun will usually be **ence**.

b. The Head Teacher thanked us for our (**comply**) with the school uniform rule.

.... **(1 mark)**

c. My (**rely**) on my brother to help me with my homework has got to stop!

.... **(1 mark)**

d. The instructions said that after the (**apply**) of glue, the two sides would stick together.

.... **(1 mark)**

e. After much (**reassure**) from my friends, I felt able to confront the bully.

.... **(1 mark)**

f. The (**disappear**) of our dog in the middle of the night was a complete mystery.

.... **(1 mark)**

4 Turn the following words into nouns by adding either the suffix **ence** or **ance**.

a. interfere .... **(1 mark)**

b. persevere .... **(1 mark)**

c. adhere .... **(1 mark)**

Suffixes from Greek

1 Write a word that includes each of the suffixes **phone**, **meter**, **logy** and **phobia**, then write its meaning. **(8 marks)**

Suffix	Word	Meaning
phone	....	....
meter	....	....
logy	....	....
phobia	....	....

Total $\frac{}{27}$

The rule 'i before e except after c but only when it rhymes with bee'

1 Write six words that follow the rule 'i before e except after c but only when it rhymes with bee'.

(6 marks)

....

....

....

2 Underline the correct spelling of the words in brackets in these sentences.

a. After searching high and low, I eventually found my (receipt / reciept).   **(1 mark)**

b. I didn't want to (decieve / deceive) my mum so I told her about the torn book.   **(1 mark)**

c. The teachers (percieved / perceived) that the child had been bullied.   **(1 mark)**

d. My dad pulled a muscle in his back while painting the (cieling / ceiling).   **(1 mark)**

e. The idea was (conceived / concieved) by the student council members.   **(1 mark)**

f. The Queen was graciously (received / recieved) by the Fijian islanders.   **(1 mark)**

Top tip!

Although it's a good idea to remember the rule 'i before e except after c but only when it rhymes with bee', you must learn the exceptions too! Here are some examples:

beige   feign   foreign   forfeit   height
neighbour   vein   weight

3 The following anagrams are exceptions to the rule 'i before e except after c, but only when it rhymes with bee'. Write the correctly spelled word next to the anagram.

a. eghit .... **(1 mark)**

b. hitweg .... **(1 mark)**

c. beegi .... **(1 mark)**

d. driew .... **(1 mark)**

e. tropien .... **(1 mark)**

f. finecafe .... **(1 mark)**

Words ending in fer

1 Add the suffixes **al**, **ence** and **ed** to the words on the left, then tick the correct box to indicate whether the **fer** sound is stressed or unstressed. **(10 marks)**

Word	Add suffixes	Is the **fer** stressed? ✓/✗
refer	**al**:...	
	ence:...	
	ed:...	
transfer	**al**:...	
	ence:...	
	ed:...	
prefer	**ence**:...	
	ed:...	
infer	**ence**:...	
	ed:...	

Total —— 28

Letter string ough

1 Complete the table with as many words as you can find containing the letter string **ough**, matching the words to the sounds indicated in the column headings. One word for each has been done for you.

(1 mark per word)

oh sound	**aw** sound	**uff** sound	**ow** sound	**o** sound
though	*bought*	*enough*	*bough*	*cough*
....	....	....	....	....
....	....	....	....	

2 The words underlined in these sentences have been spelled as they sound. Rewrite them, correcting the words by using the **ough** letter string.

a. My brother <u>brawt</u> me some <u>coff</u> medicine because he <u>thawt</u> it would make me better. **(1 mark)**

....

b. The <u>ruff</u> seas were bad <u>enuf</u> but once on land, a <u>bow</u> from a <u>tuff</u> old oak tree snapped and landed on my head. **(1 mark)**

....

Silent letters

1 Explain what is meant by a **silent letter**. **(1 mark)**

....

2 Underline the **silent letters** in the following words. **(12 marks)**

a. assign

b. debt

c. crumb

d. nestle

e. condemn

f. honest

g. foreign

h. sword

i. knowledge

j. hymn

k. scissors

l. receipt

3 The words in bold in the following sentences have had their silent letters removed. Rewrite the words using the correct spelling.

a. Last **Wenesday**, I went to buy some new **hankerchiefs** in town.　　**(1 mark)**

....　　.................................

b. Despite the **josling** crowds, I finally bought a card with a **silouette** of a flower in the corner.　　**(1 mark)**

....　　.................................

c. I put my **receit** safely in my bag and had a drink before **succuming** to the rush hour traffic.　　**(1 mark)**

....　　.................................

d. The songs we sang were quite **solem** and **ecoed** around the hall.　　**(1 mark)**

....　　.................................

The prefix psych

1 In the following words, the prefix **psych** has become separated from the rest of word, which is an anagram.
Unravel the root words and join them to the prefix **psych** to make the correct word.

a. psych gooly　...　**(1 mark)**

b. psych tristia　...　**(1 mark)**

c. psych ci　...　**(1 mark)**

d. psych delice　...　**(1 mark)**

The letters ph

1 How many words can you list that either begin with **ph** or have **ph** in them?

(up to 12 marks)

....	....	....
....	....	....
....	....	....
....	....	....

Total $\frac{}{44}$

Words ending in o

1 Write the **plurals** of the following words.   **(9 marks)**

Singular	Plural
piano	....
hero	....
mango	....
studio	....
banjo	....
echo	....
kilo	....
potato	....
torpedo	....

Words ending in f, ff and fe

1 Change the words in brackets from **singular to plural**.

a. My dad put up some new (shelf) in my bedroom.

....   **(1 mark)**

b. We had to buy some new (knife) as the old ones were blunt.

....   **(1 mark)**

c. Our (life) have changed dramatically since we got our puppy.

....   **(1 mark)**

d. All through the night we heard the howls of (wolf).

....   **(1 mark)**

e. We heard there had been (thief) in our school last night.

....   **(1 mark)**

2 Rewrite the sentences below, changing the underlined singular nouns ending in **f** or **ff** to the **plural**.

a. The tribal <u>chief</u> agreed to respect each other's different <u>belief</u>.　　**(1 mark)**

....

b. From the top of the <u>roof</u> came billowing <u>puff</u> of white smoke.　　**(1 mark)**

....

c. The pirate's <u>bluff</u> had gone on long enough so the captain dropped anchor in front of the towering white <u>cliff</u> and confronted him.　　**(1 mark)**

....

....

d. The garden party <u>chef</u> put on <u>waterproof</u> when it started to rain.　　**(1 mark)**

....

e. The little <u>waif</u> were poorly dressed and underfed after being looked after by two beastly <u>oaf</u>.　　**(1 mark)**

....

Words with two possible plurals

1 Write both plural forms of these singular nouns.　　**(4 marks)**

Singular	Plural 1	Plural 2
scarf	....	....
wharf	....	....
dwarf	....	....
hoof	....	....

Total $\overline{23}$

Homophones

1 Write a definition for the word **homophone**.　　**(1 mark)**

....

2 Each of the following sentences contains words in bold that are homophones. Tick the **one** which has used the right ones.　　**(1 mark)**

a. We weren't **aloud** to **waist** food as Mum was always very conscious of people who were starving.　☐

b. There was a **pear** of shoes on the **stares** that I had never seen before.　☐

c. I couldn't **bare** him when we were growing up but now we are **to** old to squabble.　☐

d. I looked **through** the window and saw a huge **bear** ambling about in the garden.　☐

3 Match these words up with a homophone. For some, you may find more than one.　　**(14 marks)**

Word	Homophone(s)	Word	Homophone(s)
pause	....	whether	....
piece	....	find	....
pour	....	great	....
knew	....	shore	....
buy	....	night	....
morning	....	sent	....
profit	....	root	....

4 Choose the correct word to complete each sentence below.　**(5 marks)**

a. **main / mane**

We walked down the

....

road to get to the bus stop.

b. They're / There

.... was a lot of traffic as it was rush hour.

c. due / dew

In addition, there was a hold up .... to roadworks.

d. guest / guessed

We .... that our bus would be very late.

e. proceeded / preceded

So we .... to walk to school instead.

Near homophones

1 Explain what **near homophones** are. **(1 mark)**

....

2 Circle the **correct** word in the following sentences.

  a. The hot, sunny weather had a therapeutic **effect / affect** on the whole family. **(1 mark)**

  b. The teacher gave the parents some great **advise / advice** about the tests. **(1 mark)**

  c. The fireman couldn't gain **access / excess** to the burning building. **(1 mark)**

  d. Last night the pool was full of screaming **adolescents / adolescence**. **(1 mark)**

  e. I bought the latest **edition / addition** of my favourite magazine. **(1 mark)**

  f. We all found it difficult to **accept / except** that our cat had gone. **(1 mark)**

To help you remember **practice / practise**: **practice** with a **c** is a **noun**; **c** comes before **n** in the alphabet; **practise** with an **s** is a **verb**; **s** comes before **v** in the alphabet.

This also works with **advice / advise** too!

Total $\frac{}{28}$

1 Complete the sentence with an appropriate **conjunction**. **(1 mark)**

Hassan stopped playing basketball ....
his wrist was sore.

2 Tick **one** word to make the sentence below grammatically correct. **(1 mark)**

My little brother .... when he was running in the park.

falled ☐

falls ☐

felled ☐

fell ☐

3 Which word is an **antonym** of **sensible**? Tick **one**. **(1 mark)**

lively ☐

irresponsible ☐

calm ☐

practical ☐

4 Tick the sentence that uses the correct **plural**. Tick **one**. **(1 mark)**

Did you see those womens running on the track? ☐

There were six gooses waddling down the road. ☐

The polite man stood up to let the old ladys sit down. ☐

The thieves were arrested as they tried to leave town. ☐

5 Underline the **fronted adverbial** in this sentence. **(1 mark)**

Cautiously, the boys crept into the cave, treading carefully as they went.

6 Replace the underlined words with the correct **pronoun**. **(1 mark)**

```
┌─────────────────────┐
│                     │
└──────────┬──────────┘
           │
           ▼
```

When Sonia arrived at her dad's bedside, <u>Sonia</u> could see that <u>her dad</u> had improved.

```
           ▲
           │
┌──────────┴──────────┐
│                     │
└─────────────────────┘
```

7 Label the words below as either **nouns** or **adjectives**. **(1 mark)**

```
┌─────────────┐  ┌─────────────┐
│             │  │             │
└──────┬──────┘  └──┬──────────┘
       │            │
       ▼            ▼
```

Phil studied the detailed map then put it back neatly in his waterproof rucksack.

```
       ▲                              ▲
       │                              │
┌──────┴──────┐              ┌────────┴────────┐
│             │              │                 │
└─────────────┘              └─────────────────┘
```

8 What is the function of the sentence below? Tick **one**. **(1 mark)**

What a fuss you have made about nothing!

a question ☐

a command ☐

an exclamation ☐

a statement ☐

9 **a.** Write an explanation of the word **synonym**. **(1 mark)**

....

b. Write one word that is a synonym of **tired**. **(1 mark)**

....

10 Circle the two **conjunctions** in the sentence below. **(1 mark)**

Our football team finally won but we know we have a long way to go before we can claim the league cup.

11 Tick one box in each row to show if the sentence is in the **present progressive** or the **past progressive**. **(1 mark)**

Sentence	Present progressive	Past progressive
My sisters were eating jam and toast.		
Ushma's dog was teasing my cat.		
The boys are swimming in the sea early this morning.		

12 Replace the underlined words in the sentence below with their **expanded forms**. **(1 mark)**

I've always loved the end of the summer term when the weather's sunny and we've finished our exams.

13 Circle the **conjunction** in the sentence below. **(1 mark)**

My younger brother loves peas yet hates carrots.

14 **a.** What is the name of the punctuation marks on either side of the words <u>the one from America</u> in the sentence below? **(1 mark)**

My cousin – the one from America – is always talking about celebrities.

....

b. What is the name of a different punctuation mark that could be used correctly in the same places? **(1 mark)**

....

⑮ Insert a **semi-colon** in the correct place in the sentence below. **(1 mark)**

We met a lovely family on holiday last year we are meeting up with them again this year.

⑯ Circle all the **prepositions** in the sentence below. **(1 mark)**

My dog jumped over the gate and ran into the field.

⑰ Underline the **subordinate clause** in the sentence below. **(1 mark)**

My brother went to school today, although he has his arm in plaster.

⑱ Underline the words in this sentence that tell you it is a **question**. **(1 mark)**

"So you think you're going to win the match tomorrow, do you?"

⑲ Add **inverted commas** to this dialogue. **(1 mark)**

Hurry up or you'll be late for school! shouted my mum. It's almost 9 o'clock.

⑳ **a.** Circle the word in the sentence that contains an **apostrophe** to indicate a **contraction**. **(1 mark)**

Mum has been waiting for ages for Katie's bus but it's clearly late.

b. Circle the word in the sentence that contains an **apostrophe** for **possession**. **(1 mark)**

We're thrilled that Jake's birthday celebration wasn't ruined by the bad weather.

21 Tick one box in each row to show whether the underlined clause is a **main clause** or a **subordinate clause**.   **(1 mark)**

Sentence	Main clause	Subordinate clause
Claudie went home early <u>because she was tired</u>.		
<u>Mrs Smith</u>, who used to be my teacher, <u>visited us in school today</u>.		
<u>We will go to the beach</u> if the weather improves.		

22 Which sentence is grammatically correct? Tick **one**.   **(1 mark)**

Erin's pencil case is more fuller than Sian's.   ☐

Stella's reading is more advanced than Chloe's.   ☐

Jordan's dog is more viciouser than Ahmed's.   ☐

Our homework is more harder than yours.   ☐

23 Add a **colon** to the sentence below.   **(1 mark)**

When I go away for a weekend in the countryside, I always pack the following sweaters, boots, gloves and a coat.

24 Complete the sentence using the **present perfect** form of the verb **to eat**.   **(1 mark)**

Now that we .... our breakfast, we can set off on our journey.

25 Which verb completes the sentence so that it uses the **subjunctive form**?

(1 mark)

I wish I .... better at cooking so I could help you in the kitchen when we have visitors.

Tick **one**.

did ☐

might be ☐

was ☐

were ☐

26 Which event is the **most likely** to happen? Tick **one**.

(1 mark)

I will finish my homework project this evening. ☐

Orla might be going to the library with her mum. ☐

The forecaster said that it could snow later on. ☐

I may drop your book off at around 9 o'clock. ☐

27 Use the **conjunctions** in the box to complete the sentence below. Use each conjunction **once**.

(1 mark)

but	or	even though	and

You need to water the flowers .... the plants,

.... it rained in the night. Here is a watering can

.... you might prefer to use a jug ....

a hose.

28 Circle the **subject** in the sentence below.

(1 mark)

Our house has a south-facing garden.

29 Explain the meaning of each sentence, where one has a comma and the other does not. **(1 mark)**

Shall we start to eat, Mum?

Shall we start to eat Mum?

....

....

....

30 Insert one **comma** in the correct place in the sentence below. **(1 mark)**

After an extremely long flight I was relieved to get into my comfortable bed for a sleep.

31 What does the root **graph** mean in the word family below? **(1 mark)**

bio**graph**y   photo**graph**   **graph**ics   para**graph**

Tick **one**.

write or draw ☐

speak and talk ☐

break or destroy ☐

listen or hear ☐

32 Insert a **contraction** into the sentence below. **(1 mark)**

There isn't time for us to eat because .... already 9 o'clock.

33 Put one letter in each box to show what type of word each one is. **(1 mark)**

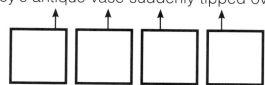

| noun
A | adverb
B | verb
C | adjective
D |

Mrs Courtney's antique vase suddenly tipped over.

↑   ↑   ↑   ↑

☐ ☐ ☐ ☐

34 Rearrange the words in the statement below to make it a question. Use only the given words. Remember to punctuate your sentence correctly. **(1 mark)**

Statement: The children are going to bed.

Question: ....

35 Put a tick in each row to show how the **apostrophe** has been used in each sentence. An example has been done for you. **(1 mark)**

Sentence	Apostrophe used in a contraction	Apostrophe used to show possession
There's not a lot of room in here.	✓	
I daren't tell the teacher I forgot my homework.		
Rebecca's pony likes apples.		
The children's books are in the library.		

36 Add a **prefix** from the box below to give this word a negative meaning.

(1 mark)

................legal

| in | il | un |

37 Complete the sentence below using the verbs in brackets in the
past progressive tense.   **(1 mark)**

As we (**walk**) .... along the beach, we saw some birds

which (**fly**) .... high in the sky.

38 Tick the word that is closest in meaning to **mishap**. Tick **one**.   **(1 mark)**

unhappiness ☐

accident ☐

distortion ☐

trick ☐

39 Underline the **two** words in the passage below that show a command.

(1 mark)

Turn to the next page and read the first two paragraphs. What do you think
made Theo react that way?

40 Insert an **apostrophe** in the sentence below to show **possession**.   **(1 mark)**

Mrs Rothwells computer screen needed to be fixed.

Active voice – The subject of the sentence is doing or being; the object is having it done to them/it

Adjective – A word that describes a noun

Adverb – A word that tells us more about a verb (how, where, when), an adjective, another adverb or a whole clause

Adverbial – A word, phrase or clause that tells us more about a verb (how, where, when, how often) or clause

Ambiguity – Having more than one meaning

Antonym – A word that means the opposite to another word

Apostrophe – A punctuation mark used to show omission (contraction) or possession

Brackets – Can show parenthesis

Bullet points – Used to draw attention to items in a list

Capital letters – Letters in upper case, used at the start of sentences and proper nouns

Clause – Contains a verb and can act as a sentence. It can be a main clause or subordinate clause

Colon – Introduces a clause that gives detail about the previous clause or introduces a list, a quotation or speech in a play script

Comma – Punctuation mark used to separate items in a list, clarify meaning, avoid ambiguity and indicate parenthesis; it can also be used in punctuating direct speech

Command – Gives an instruction

Common nouns – Nouns for people, animals and objects

Conjunction – Links two words, phrases or clauses

Contraction – A word that has been made shorter

Coordinating conjunction - Links two words, phrases or clauses of equal importance

Dash – A single dash shows a break or pause in a sentence

Dashes – Can show parenthesis

Determiner – A word that introduces a noun such as 'the', 'a', 'some' and 'those'

Dialogue – Conversation between two or more people

Direct speech – A sentence in inverted commas showing the exact words spoken by someone

Ellipsis – The omission of text, sometimes shown by three dots (...)

Emphasis – Stress

Exclamation – A sentence that shows feelings like fear, anger, happiness or excitement

Exclamation mark – Punctuation at the end of an exclamation or command

Expanded noun phrase – A phrase with a noun as its main word with other words that tell us more about that noun

Formal speech – Speaking and writing using correct grammar and vocabulary

Fronted adverbial – An adverbial that comes at the front, or start, of a sentence

Full stops – Punctuation at the end of a sentence

Homophones – Words that sound the same but have a different spelling and different meanings

Hyphen – A punctuation mark that links words to make some compound words, to join prefixes to some words or to show a word break at the end of a line

Hyphenated compound words – Two words combined with a hyphen to make one new word

Informal speech and writing – Relaxed, chatty way of speaking and writing used with family and friends

Inverted commas – The punctuation at the start and end of speech

Main clause – A clause that can make sense as a sentence

Modal verbs – Verbs that show possibility or likelihood

Noun phrase – A phrase where a noun is the main word

Nouns – Naming words for people, places, animals and things

Object – A noun, pronoun or noun phrase

Omission – Leaving letters or words out

Parentheses – The plural form of parenthesis. It can also mean the punctuation marks themselves

Parenthesis – The insertion of a word or phrase into a sentence as an explanation or afterthought

Passive voice – When the subject isn't carrying out the action but is being acted upon by someone or something

Past – A verb tense showing what has happened

Past perfect – A verb tense formed from the past tense of the verb 'have' + the past participle of the main verb

Past progressive – A verb tense showing a continuous action in the past

Glossary

Personal pronoun – A word that replaces a noun

Phrase – A group of words that work together as if they are one word

Possession – Ownership

Possessive pronoun – A word to show ownership

Possessive determiner – Shows ownership of the noun that immediately follows

Prefix – A string of letters added to the start of a word to change its meaning

Preposition – Shows the relationship between the noun or pronoun and other words in the clause or sentence

Present – A verb tense showing what is happening now

Present perfect – A verb tense formed from the present tense of the verb 'have' + the past participle of the main verb

Present progressive – A verb tense showing a continuous action in the present

Proper nouns – Nouns that name particular things. They begin with a capital letter

Punctuation marks – 'Signposts' to help us understand text

Question – A sentence that asks something

Question mark – Punctuation mark at the end of a question

Relative clause – A subordinate clause introduced by a relative pronoun

Relative pronoun – The words 'who', 'which', 'that' and 'whose' which introduce a relative clause

Root word – A word in its own right, without a prefix or a suffix

Semi-colon – Links two closely related sentences or separates items in a list where some items might be longer than one or two words

Silent letter – A letter that was once pronounced but now isn't

Standard English – Using the rules of English correctly

Statement – A sentence that gives information

Stress – When you either increase the vowel length or loudness of the syllable or both

Subject – The person or thing that is doing or being something in the sentence

Subjunctive mood – Used in formal speech and writing to express a wish or an imaginary state

Subordinate clause – A clause which depends on the main clause to make sense

Subordinating conjunction – Joins a subordinate clause to a main clause

Suffix – A string of letters added to the root word to change or add to its meaning

Syllable – A single, unbroken sound containing a vowel (or y)

Synonym – A word that means the same or almost the same as another word

Thesaurus – A book of words and their synonyms

Verb – A word for an action or state of being

ACKNOWLEDGEMENTS

The author and publisher are grateful to the copyright holders for permission to use quoted materials and images.

All images © Shutterstock.com

Every effort has been made to trace copyright holders and obtain their permission for the use of copyright material. The author and publisher will gladly receive information enabling them to rectify any error or omission in subsequent editions. All facts are correct at time of going to press.

Published by Letts Educational
An imprint of HarperCollins*Publishers*
1 London Bridge Street
London SE1 9GF

ISBN 9781844199280
This edition published 2017
10 9 8 7 6 5

© Letts Educational, an imprint of HarperCollins*Publishers* Limited 2017

All rights reserved. No part of this publication may be reproduced, stored in a retrieval system, or transmitted, in any form or by any means, electronic, mechanical, photocopying, recording or otherwise, without the prior permission of Letts Educational.

British Library Cataloguing in Publication Data.

A CIP record of this book is available from the British Library.

Series Concept and Development: Michelle I'Anson
Commissioning and Series Editor: Charlotte Christensen
Author: Shelley Welsh
Project Management and Editorial: Cambridge Publishing Management and Richard Toms
Cover Design: Amparo Barrera
Inside Concept Design: Paul Oates
Text Design and Layout: Cambridge Publishing Management
Production: Natalia Rebow
Printed at Martins The Printers Ltd